TIME IS RUNNING OUT!

Am I Really in Good Standing with God?

Daniel G. Ochoa

WESTBOW
P R E S S®
A DIVISION OF THOMAS NELSON
& ZONDERVAN

WestBow Press books may be ordered through booksellers or by contacting:

WestBow Press
A Division of Thomas Nelson & Zondervan
1663 Liberty Drive
Bloomington, IN 47403
www.westbowpress.com
844-714-3454

Scripture quotations marked NKJV are taken from the New King James Version. Copyright © 1982 by Thomas Nelson, Inc. Used by permission. All rights reserved.

Scripture quotations marked NIV are taken from the Holy Bible, New International Version®, NIV®. Copyright © 1973, 1978, 1984 by Biblica, Inc.™ Used by permission of Zondervan. All rights reserved worldwide.

ISBN: 979-8-3850-0717-2 (sc)
ISBN: 979-8-3850-0718-9 (e)

Library of Congress Control Number: 2023917381

Print information available on the last page.

WestBow Press rev. date: 01/31/2024

DEDICATION

With profound gratitude and love, I wholeheartedly dedicate this book to the three most cherished people in my life: my beloved wife, my son and my daughter. Their love and unique challenges have played an instrumental role in shaping the person I am today and the depth of my walk with Jesus.

I am also immensely grateful for the invaluable contributions of the following people, whose teachings and guidance have been the cornerstone of this book's creation:

J. Vernon McGee
C.S. Lewis
Buck Oliphant
Carter Sanger
John Piper
Matt Heard
Timothy Keller
Chuck Swindoll

Eschatology Teaching
Jared Lewis
Nelson Walters

Joel Richardson
Dalton Thomas

Apologetics Teaching
Frank Turek

Each of you has played a significant role in the realization of this project, and I am deeply humbled and thankful for your influence in my life. May this book, guided by the teachings of God through your wisdom, bring blessings and inspiration to all who read it.

WAKING UP TO THE TRUTH!

Among all the Christmases in my life, there was one that stood out vividly from the rest. It was the year 1969, and I was an eight-year-old. What made this Christmas truly remarkable was the revelation I experienced about Santa Claus. Growing up in a modest home with a mere 1,240 square feet of space and a solitary bathroom alongside my four siblings posed its challenges. However, as a child, blissfully unaware, I embraced our circumstances with contentment.

Although my parents hailed from Mexico, our family celebrated Christmas in a manner that blended Mexican traditions with those commonly practiced by American families. Yet when it came to the pivotal act of placing gifts under the Christmas tree on the magical night of Christmas Eve, my parents followed a slightly unconventional tradition. Instead of Santa Claus discreetly arranging the presents beneath the tree as depicted in countless holiday movies, he mysteriously placed them beneath our own beds. Reflecting on this distinctive approach now, I appreciate the intimate touch it brought to our Christmas experience. No longer did I need to wait patiently for everyone to awaken on Christmas morning or partake in the collective unwrapping of presents around the tree, trying to discern which ones belonged to me. Instead, the moment I awoke, the treasures hidden beneath my bed were mine alone to explore and unwrap with unbridled joy.

That particular year, I found myself grappling with the whole belief of Santa Claus. Some of my classmates, who had seemingly uncovered the truth the previous year, were now flaunting their knowledge, declaring that Santa did not exist and that our parents were the ones responsible for the gifts. It was a shocking revelation for me as I desperately clung to my belief in Santa Claus. In my confusion, I turned to the one person I knew I could trust: my mother. I approached my mother, and I asked her the question that weighed heavily on my young mind: "Is Santa Claus real?" In response, she valiantly sought to convince me of his existence, assuring me that if I stopped believing, he would cease to visit. Yet as a child, the perplexing nature of the situation left me pondering the truth.

Aware of my struggle with the whole Santa Claus ordeal, my mother approached me about two weeks before Christmas. She said, "Danny, how would you like to accompany me and your little sister to Sears department store to meet Santa Claus?"

"When?" I asked eagerly.

Her response was, "Right now." Excitedly, I agreed. She instructed me to put on my winter clothing and boots while she prepared my little sister. Once we were ready, my mother ushered us into the back seat of her car. In those days, seat belts were not a concern, so we simply hopped into the back seat and sat wherever we pleased. My mother often had to remind us to sit down so she could see through the rear window as she pulled out of the driveway. I felt a mixture of excitement and nerves because I was not sure if I had been good enough to deserve toys that year.

I did not want to meet Santa, only to discover that I was on his naughty list. So halfway to our destination, I turned to my mother and said, "Mom?"

"Qué mi hijo?" (What, my son?) Both of my parents were originally from Mexico, and at that time, their English skills were minimal. Whenever I posed a question that required a quick response, instead of struggling with her English, she found it easier to reply in Spanish. In fact, my mother learned to speak English by watching her favorite TV show *I Love Lucy*.

2

So I asked her, "Do you think I've been good enough to receive presents from Santa this year?"

She affectionately replied, "Oh, Daniel, por supuesto que has sido lo suficientemente bueno para recibir regalos este año." (Oh, Daniel, of course, you have been good enough to receive presents this year.) She reassured me that despite some minor missteps that might have upset my father and her, I had also done many good things, and she was certain that Santa would bring me some toys. Hearing those words from my mother brought immense relief and made me feel more at ease about meeting Santa.

o   o   o

Upon arriving at the Sears parking lot, my mother parked the car and opened the back door, allowing my little sister and me to step out. It was a bitterly cold day, but the layers of clothing my mother had made me bundle up in, combined with the anticipation of meeting Santa Claus, made me oblivious to the chill. Hand in hand, my mother guided us through the department store toward Santa's location.

As we entered Santa's workshop, the place was teeming with people, making it difficult for me to see much. However, I was willing to stand there indefinitely if necessary. After what felt like an eternity of waiting, we finally reached the front of the line, with only a few people ahead of us. And then I could not believe my eyes—there he was, donned in his vibrant red suit, adorned with big black boots, white gloves, and a red hat. In no time, it was our turn. As I stood there, awaiting my moment, I was awestruck. The place resembled something out of a television show. Elves scurried about, presents abounded, lights twinkled, and a resplendent Christmas tree illuminated the scene. I was rendered speechless.

As I soaked in the enchanting atmosphere, one of Santa's helpers approached us and said, "OK, it's your turn." I struggled to ascend a few steps—partly due to nerves and partly because my mother insisted on outfitting me in a one-piece snowsuit, along with oversize black boots handed down from my elder brother. To top it off, I wore one of those hats with flaps on both sides to shield my ears. Moving around with all that gear was no easy feat.

My sister and I made our way to Santa, and he greeted my little sister with a jolly "Ho ho ho! Merry Christmas! What is your name?" He lifted her onto his lap. Then he looked at me, grinned, and in a deep voice, asked, "And what is your name?"

With his assistance, I climbed onto his lap and replied, "Danny."

First, Santa turned his attention to my sister, inquiring, "And what would you like for Christmas this year?" As my sister revealed her Christmas wishes, I could not help but gaze at Santa's face in utter disbelief. All the doubts I had about Santa's existence vanished. I knew he was real because I sat on his lap, able to touch him and hear his voice. He was undeniably real.

After my sister had shared her desires, Santa then shifted his gaze toward me and asked, "Danny, what would you like for Christmas this year?" I could not recall precisely what I requested that day, but I could remember him assuring me that he would do his utmost to place it under the tree for me on Christmas morning. As he gently helped me off his knee, a thought crossed my mind. *You mean under my bed.* However, I had no intention of correcting Santa. I simply assumed that with the multitude of houses he had to visit, he must have momentarily forgotten that our house was the one where the presents were placed under our beds.

○   ○   ○

Upon returning home that evening, I could not contain my excitement as I rushed to tell my two elder brothers about our visit to see Santa Claus. I recounted how I sat on his lap, shared my Christmas wishes, and heard him promise to do his best to fulfill them. Any lingering doubt I had about Santa Claus vanished completely that year. It was astonishing how close I came to believing those kids at school who tried to convince me otherwise.

I was filled with anticipation for Christmas, even though it was just a couple of weeks away. Time seemed to crawl when you were a child.

Thinking about Christmas in January or even in the middle of summer felt like an eternity away. It was only after Thanksgiving that it started to occupy our minds. However, as we grow older, time appears to speed up, even though the number of months, days, and hours remain the same. It is as if God has embedded a mechanism within us to make us acutely aware of the brevity and preciousness of life on the earth. Hopefully, as we age, we can shift our focus toward the things that truly matter in life.

○   ○   ○

Years ago, a pastor at the church I attended in Katy, Texas, imparted a profound lesson during one of his sermons. He shared that no one on their deathbed ever expresses regrets about working harder, spending more time in the office, or chasing after promotions. Instead, the most common regrets people have at the end of their lives are centered on two fundamental aspects: wishing they had spent more time with their family and longing for more time spent immersed in God's Word.

This wisdom resonated deeply with me, and it reminded me of an encounter with the renowned evangelist Billy Graham. When asked about the biggest surprise in his life after speaking at a college, Graham responded without hesitation that the brevity of life was the most astounding realization. Despite witnessing numerous events and traveling extensively, it was the fleeting nature of existence that struck him the hardest.

Reflecting on these insights, I recognized the paradox in our pursuits. We often devote our energy and focus to ambitious goals, only to discover that they pale in comparison to what truly matters: our relationship with God and our loved ones. The words of my pastor compelled me to make a conscious decision to prioritize a life centered on God and my son over personal ambitions. I came to realize that even if I were blessed with reaching the age of eighty or ninety, life would still be remarkably short. Furthermore, there are no guarantees of another year or even tomorrow.

This realization served as a wake-up call, urging me to seize the precious moments and cherish the relationships that bring true fulfillment. It prompted me to live with an awareness of the brevity of life and the uncertainty of its duration. By aligning my priorities with eternal values, I strive to cultivate a life that encompasses love, faith, and meaningful connections.

○   ○   ○

Finally, Christmas Eve arrived, signaling that Christmas morning was just around the corner. I could hardly contain my excitement, not necessarily because of the family gathering or the true meaning of Christmas, but mainly because I could not wait to discover the toys Santa had placed under my bed. Unlike other nights when I resisted going to bed at the time my mother deemed appropriate for an eight-year-old, on this particular night, she did not have to tell me to go to bed because I was already planning on going to bed early. There is something magical about sleep. Despite sleeping for eight or ten hours during the night, it always feels like time flies by when we are asleep, as if someone has pressed the fast-forward button on the clock. I figured that if I went to bed early that night, the morning would arrive that much quicker. So at around eight o'clock, I went to inform my mother that I was ready to go to bed. With five kids in the family, she had no objections, probably thinking, *One down, four to go.*

I lay in bed, longing to fall asleep, but the excitement for Christmas prevented me from doing so. The more I thought about it, the more elusive sleep became. After about thirty minutes of restlessness, I could not resist the temptation any longer. I got up and quietly made my way downstairs. Everyone seemed to be enjoying themselves, and when my mother noticed me, she inquired about my return. I confessed that I could not fall asleep. She reminded me that Santa would not come if I was awake. That was all the motivation I needed to retreat back upstairs. I was determined not to ruin my Christmas just because sleep eluded me. I laid in bed for what felt like hours, but in reality, it was probably only about thirty minutes.

The next morning, I was the first one to rise, around six o'clock. I leaped out of bed, landing on all fours to waste no time in checking under my bed. I bent my head down and peered into the darkness, but I struggled to see clearly. Squinting, I tried to discern any signs of presents, but it appeared as though there was nothing under my bed. Uncertain, I speculated that Santa might have pushed them so far back that they were out of sight without proper lighting. Without hesitation, I sprinted to the light switch, flooding the room with brightness. Rushing back to the side of my bed, I positioned myself on all fours once again, hoping for a different outcome. To my astonishment, there was nothing under the bed—absolutely nothing.

My anxiety started to build, and a flurry of thoughts raced through my mind. Had Santa forgotten to visit our house? Or worse, were we deemed unworthy of presents? I reassured myself, recalling that my mother had affirmed my good behavior and the extra effort I had put in during the past month. As a child who believed in Santa Claus, the closer Christmas approached, the harder I strived to be good. Sometimes my elder brothers would exploit Santa's influence whenever they wanted things to go their way. In December, they would say, "You know Santa knows how you are behaving, so you better …" And then they would add whatever they desired to the end of that statement to manipulate the situation. However, they knew better than to try this tactic when Christmas was still more than a month away. At that point, I only cared about doing what was right and making an extra effort to be good when Christmas was imminent. But as the holiday drew near, I did not want to take any chances, so I always gave in to their demands.

Feeling distraught, I rushed to the other side of the room where my eldest brother, Manuel, slept. We shared the upstairs space, which was one large room, perfectly accommodating the three of us. As I checked under Manuel's bed, my heart sank when I discovered that he, too, had received nothing. I woke up both of my brothers and informed them that Santa had forgotten to visit us. I could not believe it. "Why wouldn't he come?" I asked them. They tried to console me, assuring me that there must be an explanation.

My eldest brother suggested that we all go downstairs and check if our sisters had received anything. So the three of us quietly descended the stairs and woke up our two sisters. To our dismay, there was nothing under their beds either. Filled with disappointment, we gathered in the living room, discussing how none of us had received any presents that Christmas morning. It was then that Manuel suggested that I go wake up Mom and inform her that Santa had not come. Deep down, I knew that if anyone had answers or could rectify the situation, it was Mom.

○   ○   ○

Carefully, I walked down the hallway toward my parents' bedroom door. With utmost caution, I slowly opened the door halfway and peeked inside. There, I could see my mom and dad peacefully asleep. Their bed was positioned in the middle of the back wall, with my father on the right side and my mother on the left. The door to the room opened toward where my father slept, so I had to tiptoe silently to the other side of the bed without making a sound. Even though it was Christmas, there was no way I was going to risk waking up my father. Despite having to wake up at five thirty for work every morning, he was not a morning person, and more often than not, he would awaken in a grumpy mood.

Everyone in the family knew to keep their distance from our father in the mornings. There were days when we would hear him slam cupboard doors in the kitchen as he prepared his morning coffee. In fact, there were two times during the day when I preferred not to be in the same room as my father: in the morning when he was getting ready for work and when he returned home from work. It was not an everyday occurrence, but if he had a tough day at work, he would come home in a bad mood. I never wanted to take any chances during those moments. It was safer to give him his space, even avoiding the kitchen, when he arrived home.

However, I want to clarify that my father was not a terrible father who would hit or mistreat us. On the contrary, he was a hard worker and a dedicated provider for the family. Despite not having received much education due to the early loss of both his parents, he worked diligently, often taking on overtime to earn extra money for the family.

He even took on a second job, delivering Mexican food to small grocery stores and restaurants on his days off. Sometimes he would take me along, and I cherished those moments. It was during those outings that I saw him not only as my father but also as a businessman, and I looked up to him with admiration. Yet on those mornings when he woke up in a bad mood, his face would bear a piercing expression that could freeze anyone in their tracks, much like the gaze of the mythical Greek god Medusa.

With great care, I tiptoed around the bed, making my way to where my mother was sleeping. As I stood next to her, I could see that she was sound asleep. I gently shook her shoulder, whispering, "Mom, Mom, Santa did not come."

Still half asleep, she slowly awakened; then it struck her. Her eyes opened wide like a deer stuck in headlights. Sitting halfway up, she urgently asked, "Where are your brothers and sisters?"

I replied, "They're in the living room." She instructed me to go back to the living room, assuring me that she would join us shortly. I obeyed, returning to the living room, where my brothers and sisters were eagerly waiting. I informed them that Mom had asked us to wait for her there and that she would be out in a few minutes.

o o o

A couple of minutes later, my mother finally emerged from her bedroom. She reassured us not to worry and explained that Santa had not forgotten our house. As she spoke, she looked toward the visible stars that led upstairs from where we were standing. With a sense of purpose, she instructed us all to gather in the kitchen and walked with us until we were all standing there. With a serious tone, she warned us not to leave the kitchen until she returned, making sure we understood her instructions. We all answered in unison, "Yes, Mom."

Given that our house was small, we could hear our mother's footsteps as she ascended the stairs to our bedroom. However, we soon noticed another sound—a creaking noise that signaled the opening of the attic door. Confused, I stood in the kitchen, wondering why my mother was heading to the attic. As any curious eight-year-old would do when their mother told them not to leave a room, I left the room and decided to take a quick peek up the stairs. To my astonishment, I witnessed my mother, dressed in her pajamas, taking out all the presents from the attic one by one. It turned out that she had forgotten to place the presents under our beds on Christmas Eve night.

Instead of merely bringing down the presents and explaining that she found them in the attic, my mother (bless her heart) carefully placed them under our beds, thinking that perhaps we had overlooked them the first time. As we stood there in the kitchen, she orchestrated this act of surprise, hoping to make amends for her forgetfulness.

As I stood there with my siblings, a thought crossed my mind—could it be true? Could all the rumors I heard from some kids at school and in the neighborhood about Santa not being real be accurate? Were my mom and dad the ones buying our Christmas presents? I looked up at my elder brother, curiosity in my eyes, and asked him directly, "So Santa isn't real?"

He smirked and replied, "I think you're old enough to know the truth. There is no Santa Claus; Mom and Dad are Santa."

Surprised by his answer, I said, "Really? There is no Santa Claus?" He affirmed my suspicion, just as our mother walked back into the kitchen.

She overheard our conversation and chimed in, suggesting that maybe we had not looked closely enough. She encouraged us to go and take another look under our beds. As I ascended the stairs, a mix of emotions ran through me. I turned to my brother and recounted my recent visit to see Santa, where I had sat on his lap and spoken with him. But my other brother, Sam, interjected, explaining that those were just men dressed up to look like Santa. He challenged me, asking if I truly believed Santa could deliver presents to every house worldwide in one night. Confused and somewhat disillusioned, I could not comprehend why so many people put in so much effort to make children believe in something that was not real and, moreover, why my parents went along with this.

That night, my mother sat me down and shared with me the true story of Christmas. It was not about Santa Claus; it was about God and his Son, Jesus. Although her understanding of the scriptures was very limited, she conveyed the basic essence of what many people believe. Reflecting on this, I found it peculiar that for so many years, my mother wanted me to believe in a Santa who was not real. She went to great lengths, taking me to department stores to see him in person, sit on his lap, and have conversations with him. And now she wanted me to believe in someone I could not see, touch, or converse with. I could not imagine this was part of God's plan.

So, for the next twenty-five years or so, I could say that I believed in God, but my perception of him was akin to that of Santa Claus. As long as I tried to be good, I was in good standing with him. The only way to end up on his naughty list was by committing something truly terrible, something that would make headlines on the front page of a newspaper.

o   o   o

It is disheartening to witness how our country has lost sight of the true meaning of Christmas. We dedicate more time to putting up decorations unrelated to Christmas than to contemplating the next chapter we should read from the Bible. We spend so much energy thinking about what presents to buy for our loved ones that we neglect to reflect on the gift God has given us.

Driving through neighborhoods during the Christmas season, one can see all kinds of unrelated decorations—Charlie Brown, the Simpsons, Santa Claus, and reindeers.

Even many Nativity displays are inaccurate. Regrettably, I must share that there were no wise men present at the birth of Christ. They arrived two or three years later, and the exact number of wise men remains unknown.

Through television and radio, we have been bombarded with the notion that Christmas revolves around Santa and other elements detached from its true essence. Consequently, we have convinced ourselves that Christmas is about the trivial things we engage in each year. If we are honest with ourselves, we have transformed Christmas into a celebration of ourselves rather than of Christ. It has become a day when everyone is celebrated, including ourselves, and we become stressed, preoccupied with what to buy for others while wondering what we will receive in return. We even adjust the amount we spend on someone based on how much they have spent on us the previous year. It is no wonder there is so much stress during the Christmas holiday— imagine celebrating everyone's birthday on the same day. At times, I ponder what God thinks as he observes how we celebrate the gift of his Son, the greatest gift bestowed on humankind.

On Christmas Eve, most families gather to read "'Twas the Night before Christmas" to their children rather than reading the true story of Christmas from the scriptures. I wish my parents had read the true story of Christmas to me from the Bible. I wish that after reading the story, we could have gathered as a family in the living room and discussed how the shepherds must have felt when the angels appeared to them or what emotions they experienced upon seeing the Christ child.

○　○　○

In today's world, it appears that many people attending church have a limited understanding of who God truly is and what he is actively doing in the world. There is a pressing need for people to awaken to the profound truth about God's nature and what it genuinely means to be a follower of Christ. I prefer using the term *follower of Christ* over *Christian*. The term *Christian* has lost its impact and significance as it is often perceived as merely believing in the God of the Bible and striving to be a good person.

However, to identify oneself as a follower of Christ signifies a deep commitment to follow the path and teachings of Jesus. Even the word *believe* has lost its weight in contemporary times compared with centuries ago. Nowadays believing often implies a mere hopeful anticipation, such as believing a particular team will win the Super Bowl. Yet in centuries past, declaring belief in God meant a wholehearted conviction, to the extent that one would be willing to sacrifice their life for that belief.

Believing in something involves action. If I say I believe in Advil, it means I use it for pain. In Acts 16:31, when the jailer asked Paul how to be saved, Paul responded: "Believe in the Lord Jesus, and you will be saved—you and your household." To believe in the Lord means embracing all that He taught.

It is crucial for people today to reexamine their understanding of God and embrace a genuine commitment to follow Christ's ways. We must grasp the profound depth of what it means to be a follower of Christ and allow it to transform our lives. It is not merely a matter of passive belief but also an active dedication to live according to the teachings and example of Jesus with wholehearted devotion and unwavering faith.

$$\circ \qquad \circ \qquad \circ$$

To truly understand and appreciate the true story of Christmas, we must journey back to the very beginning—the time of creation. In the book of Genesis, Moses enlightens us about how God has brought forth all things. It is awe inspiring to think that God has simply spoken, and creation has come into being. Such power and authority instill in me a fear of him, but as I have come to know him, it is a reverential fear, a good fear.

In Genesis 2, when Moses described the creation of man, he revealed that God took a different approach than with other creatures. Genesis 2:7 told us that God formed man from the dust of the ground. Unlike other aspects of creation that were spoken into existence, God deliberately formed man from the dust of the ground according to his desire. But God did something even more exceptional with man.

Genesis 2:7 stated that God not only formed man from the dust of the ground but also breathed into his nostrils the breath of life, and man became a living being. God breathed life into us, infusing us with an eternal soul, enabling us to commune with him for eternity. God bestowed a portion of himself in us.

That is why in Genesis 1:26 (NIV), it is written, "Then God said, 'Let us make mankind in our image, in our likeness.'" God has created us in his own likeness, sharing a resemblance with him. In the movie *The Green Mile*, there is a poignant scene where the character Paul, played by Tom Hanks, is explaining to a woman at a retirement home why he has lived so long, way beyond old age. He then explains how John Coffey (who was on death row for a crime he did not commit) had to share a part of himself with Paul to reveal his innocence. When the woman in the retirement home asks if Coffey has infected him with life, Paul responds, "Well, I guess that's a good way to put it. Yes, he infected me with life." In a similar sense, when God breathed life into us, he gave us a part of himself to make us in his likeness. Instead of viewing it as an infection, I prefer to see it as a gift. God has bestowed in us the precious gift of an eternal soul.

Moreover, God bestowed another gift on us—the gift of free will. He placed Adam and Eve in the Garden of Eden and gave them the freedom to enjoy the fruits of all the trees except one—the tree of knowledge, the tree of good and evil.

In Genesis 2:15–17 (NKJV), it is written:

> Then the Lord God took the man and put him in the garden of Eden to tend and keep it. And the Lord God commanded the man, saying, "Of every tree of the garden you may freely eat; but of the tree of the knowledge of good and evil you shall not eat, for in the day that you eat of it you shall surely die."

God granted Adam and Eve the freedom to choose, to exercise their will within the bounds of his commandment. It was an opportunity for them to demonstrate their love, trust, and obedience to God.

This sets the stage for understanding the true meaning of Christmas—the incredible story of God's love, his plan for redemption, and the gift of his Son, Jesus Christ.

God had given Adam the freedom to enjoy all the trees in the garden except for the tree of knowledge of good and evil. However, Adam and Eve were persuaded by Satan and chose to disobey God's command and ate from the forbidden tree. As a result, two types of death occurred. One was a physical death that would happen years later, marking the end of their earthly lives. The other was an immediate spiritual death—a separation from God. Their eternal souls were no longer in harmony with God, leading to their expulsion from the perfect dwelling place of God's presence, the Garden of Eden.

The Garden of Eden symbolized a place of perfect communion between God and humanity. Yet due to their sin, Adam and Eve could no longer dwell with God in that state of perfection. God, being perfect, could not turn a blind eye to their disobedience. Thus, they were barred from reentering the garden.

○   ○   ○

Now let us clarify the nature of sin. While society distinguishes various levels of wrongdoing and criminal offenses, when it comes to sinning against God, it is essentially rebellion—going against God's commands and doing what he has explicitly instructed us not to do. Sin involves humans taking matters into their own hands, making decisions about what is right and wrong without submitting to God's guidance. Adam and Eve's act of eating the fruit from the forbidden tree, though seemingly insignificant, was a direct violation of God's commandment regarding the tree of knowledge. It was their disobedience that led to their expulsion and introduced death into the world.

One common misconception is that humans must earn their way to heaven. However, through my years of witnessing to people, I have found with young people that the problem lies not in thinking we must earn our way to heaven but rather in believing we must earn our way to hell. The prevailing notion is that to go to hell, one must commit a heinous act that will warrant God's condemnation.

This idea is reminiscent of the concept of Santa Claus, where we fear being on the naughty list for committing something terrible.

Hollywood even perpetuates this notion in movies such as *Ghost* or those portraying deals with Satan. However, we must recognize that we are all born sinners. We cannot meet God's standards or uphold his commandments. Similar to Adam and Eve, we have rebelled against God, and our souls initially belong to Satan due to our rebellious nature. If going to heaven is a mere act of being good, then there will have been no need for Jesus to die on the cross.

The crux of the matter lies in the fact that we cannot attain salvation or earn our way to heaven through our actions. Instead, it is solely through the boundless grace of God and the sacrificial gift of his Son, Jesus Christ, that we find redemption and eternal life. This core distinction sets Christianity apart from all other religions, which often incorporate aspects of human nature into their teachings.

In all other religions, the notion of rewards for good deeds and punishment for wrongdoings makes logical sense as it aligns with human thinking. However, Christianity challenges this perspective by revealing that its source is not human but divine. Consequently, many people might find it difficult to accept or be attracted to its teachings. The uniqueness of Christianity lies in its resolute proclamation that salvation is a gift bestowed on us by God's grace alone, an unattainable treasure through our efforts or merits.

While other religious paths might emphasize the pursuit of self-achieved righteousness, Christianity humbly acknowledges that no human deeds or works can suffice to earn such a gift. It is a matter of divine love, unmerited favor, and the unparalleled sacrifice of Jesus Christ that paves the way to salvation for those who embrace this faith. Embracing Christianity is, in essence, acknowledging our dependence on God's grace, recognizing our imperfections, and humbly accepting the gift of eternal life that transcends our own abilities or accomplishments.

○   ○   ○

The story of Christmas encompasses God's profound love for humanity, his plan of redemption, and the gift of Jesus as the ultimate sacrifice to reconcile us with God. It is through faith in Jesus and accepting his gift of salvation that we can find forgiveness for our sins and experience true fellowship with God.

When Adam and Eve made the fateful choice to eat from the tree of knowledge, God was faced with three options. Firstly, he could have destroyed everything and reverted to the state before the creation of the universe. Secondly, he could have chosen to wipe everything out and start anew. However, instead of opting for either of these two paths, God made the extraordinary decision to redeem us. And for that, I am immensely grateful.

In the movie *The Chronicles of Narnia*, there is a powerful scene where the Witch confronts Aslan about the betrayal of Edmund, who has committed a sin. As Edmund confesses his wrongdoing to Aslan, the White Witch (which references Satan) arrives, seated on her throne, carried by a group of criminals. Descending from her throne, she claims that the traitor belongs to her, stating, "According to the law, all traitors belong to me." In response, Aslan asserts, "Don't speak to me about the law. I was there when it was written."

It would be crucial to grasp that the laws governing the universe, such as the speed and direction of Earth's rotation and its orbit around the sun, were established by God when he spoke them into existence. When God commanded Adam and Eve not to eat from the tree of good and evil, warning them that they would surely die, it became a law. You might wonder why such a severe punishment was imposed for a seemingly small sin. However, was it truly a small sin?

The Bible teaches us that God is eternal and infinite. He has always existed and will continue to exist without end. What sets God apart from everything else in creation, whether on Earth or in the galaxies above, is that everything else depends on something else for its existence. God, on the other hand, relies solely on himself for his existence. This is why when Moses asked God at the burning bush, "Who shall I say sent me?" God replied, "Tell them I AM has sent you," signifying that he has always been and always will be—he is God. This divine self-existence is what makes God holy and glorious as nothing else in creation can rely on itself for its own existence.

When God has created humanity, he bestowed on us a part of himself, the eternal soul. When we sin, which is to rebel against an eternal God, our sin becomes an eternal offense. Therefore, the only punishment for an infinite offense is an infinite punishment—a payment for our rebellion that lasts for eternity.

○　○　○

Many people prefer to believe that a person must commit something horribly wrong to go to hell. They find it difficult to accept that a single seemingly insignificant sin can have such consequences. Let us examine the story of Noah's ark, a story known universally. When people think of this story, they often perceive it as a charming narrative where Noah builds an ark, and animals board two by two. I have even seen nursery rooms adorned with this theme for newborn babies. However, this is not merely a cute story.

The truth behind the story is that God was filled with anger toward the world. Apart from Noah and his family, no one had genuine faith in God. Everyone was living for their own pleasures without considering any potential consequences. And what did God do? He destroyed everyone. How? He sent a flood—a devastating way to perish in my opinion. Imagine the terror that gripped people's minds as the water began to rise. Until that point, they had never experienced rain. They would climb to the top of their houses, hoping to be safe, but the water kept surging. They might have then sought refuge in trees, thinking they were high enough, yet the water continued its advance. And when they found themselves submerged, with nothing to hold on to, they struggled to gasp for air. But after spending too long in the water, their lives came to an end.

Consider all the families who observed Noah building the ark for all those years. Surely, there were moments when families gathered around the dinner table, and a wife would ask her husband, "Darling, what do you think about this man Noah building an ark? Do you think God will truly send a flood and wipe out everyone?"

And the husband would reply, "My dear, God is a loving God. He will not harm us. After all, we are good people. We haven't done anything to deserve something like that."

This is how people think even today. They focus solely on the notion that God is loving (which he certainly is; in fact, the Bible is the only source that clearly states this), but they need to awaken to the truth that God is also a God of justice.

Do you truly believe that every person in Noah's time was a notorious criminal? Of course not. However, none of them lived a life marked by genuine faith in God, except for Noah and his family. Did the people deserve such a fate? According to God's law, yes. Do I believe they deserved it? No, but then again, I am not God. Ultimately, your salvation and mine are not determined by what I think but by what God has done through his son Jesus Christ and our faith in him. It always fascinates me when I encounter someone who claims to be a Christian and is asked for their opinion on a matter. Instead of responding, "Well, I think it's OK," they should say, "It does not matter what I think. Let us explore what the Bible says about it."

o   o   o

Let us imagine being at a baseball game where a batter from the opposing team hits a ball down the third base line. The third baseman dives for the ball, makes a spectacular catch, quickly gets up, and throws it to first. The batter is called out, but it is a very close call, making it hard to determine if he is truly out. The replay is shown on the big screen, and it becomes clear that he is out by about a foot.

Now picture the manager of the opposing team going out to talk to the first base umpire. Their conversation is inaudible, but the manager is pleading with the umpire to cut the batter some slack. He explains how the batter has been struggling, having gone hitless in the last twenty-five at bats. The manager highlights the batter's commendable charity work with the homeless and elderly and how he prioritizes spending time with his family after each game. Additionally, the batter has four children, two of whom are adopted, with one being disabled.

After hearing all this, the umpire feels sympathetic toward the batter and decides to reverse the call. However, we all know that such a decision will be unfair. It will create a precedent and open a Pandora's box for other umpires in the league. We understand in the context of sports that rules should be treated as law, and umpires or referees should not bend them based on personal feelings or circumstances. Yet when it comes to God's law, why do some believe that he should bend the rules according to our subjective preferences?

○   ○   ○

It amuses me when people say, "When I get to heaven, the first thing I'll ask God is why he didn't do this or that." Trust me, when we stand before God (including myself), and we see his glory and all the sins we have committed against him, we will be humbled. In that moment, we will realize the many things we should have done but failed to do.

Some may question why God cannot simply overlook the little sins we commit, arguing they are not severe. We must understand that God is perfect. If he were to ignore or turn a blind eye to any sin, no matter how small it may seem to us, he would no longer be perfect. A perfect judge cannot dismiss someone's guilt based on a technicality, or we will deem them an unjust judge. Sadly, we do have flawed judges like that in our court systems.

Imagine being on trial for a crime you have not committed and discovering that the judge assigned to your case is corrupt and likely to side with the prosecutor. You will rightly object, seeking a judge who upholds the law. I do not want a God who is imperfect, who selectively ignores certain sins while addressing others. I am grateful that God is perfect. We may desire a God who conforms to our lifestyle, allowing us to do as we please, but as a wise pastor has once said, "There is a God who is and a God we want, and they are not the same. However, there is a God who is and a God we need, and they are one and the same."

Many people envision a God akin to Santa Claus, where only heinous acts like murder or rape will warrant damnation to hell. As a precaution, some people try to make amends toward the end of their lives, especially around October, November, or December, hoping to secure a place on the good list.

In summary, just as we recognize the importance of upholding rules in a sporting event, we should acknowledge that God's law is not subject to our personal feelings or desires. God's perfection and adherence to justice should be embraced, rather than seeking a God who accommodates our preferences. The only time we want a God who will bend the rules is when we think it benefits us. It is essential to remind ourselves that the rules and regulations set forth by God are not intended to exclude us from the garden but to ensure our place within it.

O   O   O

Now let us talk about the true Christmas story. About two thousand years ago, in a world tainted by the consequences of human sin, a great separation existed between humankind and God. This separation cast a shadow over the hearts and souls of all people; those who believed were yearning for a way to bridge the gap between their fallen nature and the perfection of the divine.

In the Old Testament, the people sought to reconcile with God through sacrifices according to God's law. They would bring forth innocent animals, whose blood would be shed on the altar as an offering to atone for their sins. The rituals were carried out meticulously, and the high priest, clad in sacred garments, would take the blood and sprinkle it on the tablets bearing the holy commandments. This act symbolized a temporary covering of their transgressions, a temporary restoration of fellowship with God.

However, these sacrifices could only serve as a representative solution, for the stain of sin persisted in the hearts of humanity. The cycle of offering sacrifices and seeking forgiveness would repeat, but true redemption remained elusive. Those who believed in God longed for a more permanent and profound solution to heal the brokenness and restore the relationship between God and humankind.

And so in the fullness of time, a miracle occurred—a gift of immeasurable magnitude was bestowed on humanity. God, in his infinite love and mercy, sent his only Son through a virgin birth, Jesus, into the world. Jesus, fully divine and fully human, willingly embraced the mission of redemption.

He embarked on a humble journey, born into a lowly manger in Bethlehem, surrounded by the warmth of humble shepherds, and later adored by wise men who recognized the significance of his arrival. Jesus grew in wisdom and stature, and as he reached the pinnacle of his earthly ministry, his purpose became clear: to become the ultimate sacrifice, the perfect Lamb of God, whose blood would be shed once and for all for the sins of the world.

○   ○   ○

In those days, King Herod, filled with jealousy and fear, sought to thwart the rise of this new ruler. In his desperate attempt to eliminate any potential threat to his reign, Herod resorted to unspeakable cruelty. He issued a command that struck terror into the hearts of parents in the town of Bethlehem. Every child two years old or younger was to be mercilessly slaughtered. Imagine the unimaginable pain and anguish that filled the air as soldiers invaded homes, snatching innocent babies from their mothers' arms and carrying out their ruthless orders.

Yet amid the darkness and despair, there was a glimmer of hope. Before the horrific events unfolded, an angel of the Lord had appeared to Joseph in a dream. The heavenly messenger, with a voice filled with urgency and compassion, warned Joseph of the impending danger. He instructed Joseph to take the child and Mary and flee to Egypt, seeking refuge from Herod's wrath.

Could you fathom the heaviness that burdened Joseph's heart as he witnessed the atrocity unfolding around him? Can you envision the tears streaming down his face as he held the precious child in his arms, knowing that the lives of countless others were being extinguished? It was a time of unspeakable sorrow and grief, a time when the darkness of humanity's fallen state manifested itself in its most chilling form.

Yet within this darkness, there was also a divine light that guided and protected. Joseph heeded the angel's warning, and in the dead of night, he fled with Mary and the child to a foreign land. Their journey to Egypt became a symbol of hope and deliverance—a testament to the indomitable spirit of a family driven by faith and entrusted with a sacred mission.

○　○　○

In their exile far from their homeland, Joseph and his family found solace and safety. They would remain in Egypt until the time was right, until the threat had passed. The land that once served as a refuge for Joseph and Mary would become a temporary home for the infant who would grow up to be the Savior of the world.

The events surrounding King Herod's ruthless act revealed the depth of human depravity and the lengths to which those in power would go to protect their own interests. But even in the face of such evil, God's providence and protection were at work. The angel's warning, the family's flight, and their eventual return to fulfill a divine purpose all served as a testament to the power of God's plan and his unwavering commitment to the salvation of humanity.

This somber chapter in the Christmas story reminds us of the fragility of life and the brokenness of our world. It calls us to reflect on the immense sacrifice that God himself has made, sending his Son to be the ultimate sacrifice for our sins. In the midst of the darkness, there is a flicker of hope, a promise of redemption, and an invitation to embrace the true meaning of Christmas—the birth of a Savior who will one day bring light to a world consumed by darkness.

In the final moments of his life, Jesus carried the weight of the world's sins on his shoulders. Nailed to a rugged cross, he bore the agony and torment, enduring a suffering beyond measure. As his blood was shed, the ultimate price was paid, and the veil that separated humanity from the presence of God was torn in two.

Through Jesus's sacrificial death, a new covenant was established—a covenant that did not rely on the temporary sacrifices of animals but on the eternal, unblemished blood of the Son of God. His sacrifice became the ultimate payment for the sins of all humanity, past, present, and future. The Old Testament prophecies were fulfilled, and the promise of everlasting reconciliation was realized.

The true meaning of Christmas lies in this profound act of love and sacrifice. It is a reminder that God has seen the plight of his creation and, in his unwavering grace, provided a way for restoration and eternal life. Christmas is not merely a celebration of a sweet and sentimental story; it is a testament to the depths of God's love and his unwavering commitment to reconcile with his beloved children.

○   ○   ○

I find it fascinating to note the description provided by Luke when he recounts the birth of Jesus. In Luke 2:12 (NKJV), he writes, "And this will be the sign to you: you will find a Babe wrapped in swaddling clothes, lying in a manger." Luke's choice of words captures our attention. He specifically mentions that the babe, referring to Jesus, was wrapped in swaddling clothes. This detail emphasizes the humble circumstances surrounding Jesus's birth and the simplicity of the manger where he was laid.

The act of wrapping the babe in swaddling clothes carries symbolic significance. It signifies the care and tenderness with which Mary and Joseph have handled their newborn child as swaddling clothes were used to provide warmth, security, and comfort to infants. It also highlights the humility of Jesus's entry into the world as he, the Son of God, has willingly embraced the limitations and vulnerability of human existence. It also displays that the gift from God has been intentionally wrapped, just how we wrap a present for someone. It is like me saying, "You will find your gift in a box wrapped under the tree." So when has the gift been unwrapped? Let us turn to scripture for insight.

> When the soldiers crucified Jesus, they took his clothes, dividing them into four shares, one for each of them, with the undergarment remaining. This garment was seamless, woven in one piece from top to bottom.
>
> "Let's not tear it," they said to one another. "Let's decide by lot who will get it."

This happened that the scripture might be fulfilled that said,

"They divided my clothes among them and cast lots for my garment." (John 19:23–24, NKJV)

In all four of the Gospels, it is mentioned how Jesus's garments were removed and divided, signifying the unwrapping of the gift. The gift from God, represented by the baby Jesus, was ultimately unveiled at the cross. The true gift is Jesus on the cross, bearing the weight of our sins.

O O O

Let us take a moment to reflect and understand that my intention is not to diminish the joy of Christmas decorations and gift giving, which many of us, including myself, enjoy. However, as we gather together on Christmas morning, it is crucial to remember the profound significance of the greatest gift of all—the gift of salvation through Jesus Christ. In the midst of the festivities, let us wholeheartedly embrace the true essence of Christmas, finding immense joy in the hope and redemption that his birth embodies. Above all, let us make a deliberate effort to share this profound truth with our children, nurturing within them a deep understanding of the meaning behind this joyous season.

As we prepare for the upcoming Christmas, let us also ponder the idea of redirecting a portion of our usual Christmas spending (25 to 50 percent) toward those who are truly in need. Is not this reflective of God's own actions toward us? He has not granted us our fleeting desires, for they often fall short of what we truly require. Instead, he has bestowed on us what we truly need—the gift of his Son. By extending a helping hand to those less fortunate, we embody the spirit of love, compassion, and generosity that lies at the heart of the Christmas message.

In doing so, we align ourselves with God's selfless act of grace and love. By prioritizing the needs of others, we honor the true meaning of Christmas and demonstrate our gratitude for the immeasurable gift we have received. May our actions be a testament to our faith, and may they inspire others to find joy in giving and sharing during this sacred season.

On Christmas morning, I can confidently express that there is nothing I truly need. While there may be things I want, I have come to realize that my genuine necessities are already fulfilled. I am sure that most of you reading this find that this statement is true for you as well.

○   ○   ○

As we delve into this Christmas story depicting Jesus's character, we are indeed confronted with his profound love, sacrificial nature, and selfless prioritization of others above himself. It is within this context that the book of Philippians, in chapter 2, sheds light on the mindset we ought to cultivate in our relationships with one another—an attitude akin to that of Christ Jesus. The passage eloquently states:

In your relationships with one another, have the same mindset as Christ Jesus:

> Who, being in very nature God,
> did not consider equality with God something to be
> used to his own advantage;
> rather, he made himself nothing
> by taking the very nature of a servant,
> being made in human likeness.
> And being found in appearance as a man,
> he humbled himself
> by becoming obedient to death—
> even death on a cross! (Philippians 2:5–7, NIV)

These verses serve as a reminder that Jesus has experienced two forms of death—for himself and for our sins—each displaying his unwavering commitment to us. In light of this truth, we are presented with two distinct paths we can choose to follow: a life oriented toward self or a life offered for the sake of others. It is with this call to embody the mindset of Christ Jesus that these verses begin their exhortation.

By embracing the same attitude demonstrated by Jesus, we are invited to shed the trappings of self-centeredness and instead adopt a disposition of humility, servanthood, and obedience. We are beckoned to live lives marked by self-sacrifice, mirroring the very essence of Jesus's character.

May we continuously seek to align our thoughts, words, and actions with the example set by Christ, willingly sacrificing our own desires and ambitions for the sake of others. In doing so, we not only honor his sacrificial love but also find fulfillment in living out the true essence of his teachings.

Having delved into the true Christmas story, it becomes evident that God encompasses a multitude of admirable attributes. We witness his boundless love, profound compassion, sacrificial nature, and yes, even his remarkable tolerance—all of which he demonstrates despite our inherent sinfulness. Romans 5:8 (NIV) encapsulates this truth:

> But God demonstrates his own love for us in this: While we were still sinners, Christ died for us.

o   o   o

Around twenty years ago, I started a personal tradition that I learned from Pastor Matt to help me stay focused on the true meaning of Christmas amid the busyness and distractions of the holiday season. I visited the hardware store and purchased a box of wood floor nails. I chose wood floor nails because they closely resembled the nails that might have been used on Jesus during that time. On the day after Thanksgiving, I place three nails in my pocket, so whenever I reach into my pocket for any reason, I'd feel the presence of those nails. It served as a reminder to pause and reflect on the profound meaning of the gift of Christmas, the immense sacrifice that Jesus endured on the cross for me.

This simple act allows me to keep the true essence of Christmas alive in my heart amid the hustle and bustle of the holiday season. It helps me remember the unwrapped gift, the ultimate expression of God's love and grace.

However, it is crucial for us to awaken to the truth about the other facet of God—the God of justice. As you progress beyond this chapter, I urge you to pause for a moment and delve into the profound significance of the seven seals described in the book of Revelation, commencing in chapter 6. As you immerse yourself in the accounts of how each seal unleashes horrific events upon the earth, you begin to grasp that it is Jesus himself who opens these seals, signifying his return, accompanied by his righteous wrath.

At this point, some may wonder if God in his grace will whisk his people away before these events unfold. The popular "Left Behind" books and movies have fueled this idea among millions of Believers. I want you to consider three eye-opening truths around this topic.

1. You may or may not know that there is a battle going on with Satan and all his fallen angels and God. Reflect on whether Satan's strategy will be more effective in deceiving people by convincing them that they will have to experience horrific days of the great tribulation, only to pleasantly surprise them as they are removed beforehand, or by convincing them that they will be raptured prior, only to find themselves unprepared—both physically and mentally—when they must endure these tribulations.

2. I have heard pastors using an analogy of a bride being beaten up before her wedding as an example. They question why God will allow his bride to endure such hardship. While this analogy may seem appealing, it overlooks the true essence of a bride's preparation for her wedding day. We all recognize that a bride appears most beautiful on her wedding day, and much effort and planning go into her appearance. She may engage in months of preparation, such as dieting or exercising, and on the day itself, there are numerous people assisting with hair, makeup, and dressing. So when pastors ask why God will permit his bride to be beaten up before the wedding, it seems understandable. However, what these pastors forget is God does not focus on external appearances; rather, he examines the heart.

   As stated in 1 Samuel 16:7 (NIV), "But the Lord said to Samuel, 'Do not consider his appearance or his height, for I have rejected him. The Lord does not look at the things people look at. People look at the outward appearance, but the Lord looks at the heart.'" Therefore, it is essential to explore what occurs internally when a person experiences persecution.

Let us turn to the words of Paul in the book of Romans. Romans 5:1–5 (NIV) conveys, "Therefore, since we have been justified through faith, we have peace with God through our Lord Jesus Christ, through whom we have gained access by faith into this grace in which we now stand. And we boast in the hope of the glory of God. Not only so, but we also glory in our sufferings because we know that suffering produces perseverance; perseverance, character; and character, hope. And hope does not put us to shame because God's love has been poured out into our hearts through the Holy Spirit, who has been given to us."

According to this verse, God does not beat up his bride; instead, he prepares her for the wedding day. Therefore, I find it rather silly to equate persecution with beating up the bride. Persecution serves as a means of refining and strengthening the character of believers. It fosters perseverance, develops their character, and instills hope. Ultimately, God's love is poured into their hearts through the Holy Spirit, empowering them to endure and overcome challenges. It makes sense that the hearts of those who are still here when he returns need to be fully prepared for his return. Bear in mind that our closest resemblance to Jesus is often witnessed when we stand unwavering in our faith, in the midst of suffering.

3. It is crucial to acknowledge another perspective on this matter. There are millions of Christians who are currently facing persecution to the point of death across the globe. This raises a significant question: why does God allow so many people to be killed for their beliefs, but when tribulation comes to the rest of us like Revelation tells us, we believe that God will rescue us from it? The answer lies in our context of living in America and other parts of the world where we live in comfort.

There is a statement made by a pastor that resonates with this topic. He has pointed out that when followers of Christ in third world countries encounter hardships, their prayers are for

God to give them strength to endure those difficulties. On the other hand, when Americans face challenges, their prayers tend to focus on asking God to remove those difficulties entirely.

This disparity in prayer reflects the contrasting environments in which believers find themselves. In places of great suffering, believers understand that their faith may lead them into hardships or even death, and yet their prayers reflect a desire for God's strength to navigate through those tribulations. However, in a land of relative comfort like America, there is a tendency to seek an immediate removal of hardships rather than embracing them as opportunities for growth and spiritual endurance. So why do we think that we derive better than those who risk their lives every day to be a follower of Christ?

This disparity highlights the importance of perspective and the influence of our surroundings on our faith. It is essential for us to broaden our understanding and learn from the experiences of our persecuted brothers and sisters worldwide who demonstrate unwavering faith in the midst of severe trials. Knowing this, we learn that persecution is not the wrath of God; the wrath of God is his judgment, which comes at the end of the tribulation.

In the world we inhabit today, as we approach what many believe to be the final days, I believe it becomes increasingly crucial for us to begin implementing the practice of asking God for strength when we encounter difficulties.

Now some of you may be curious about how my mother could have forgotten to place the presents under our bed on Christmas Eve night. Well, the truth of the matter only came to light years later when she finally shared the story with us. As I mentioned earlier, we had guests over that night, and my mother, not being accustomed to drinking, indulged in a glass of spiked eggnog. She confessed that the festive beverage had an unexpected effect on her, leaving her slightly tipsy. Once our guests departed, all she wanted was to retire to bed, and in the midst of her drowsiness, she completely forgot that it was Christmas Eve.

CHAPTER 2

CHANGING THE ROAD I AM ON

When I was fifteen years old, my parents made the decision to move from Lincoln Park, Michigan, to a neighboring city called Taylor. It turned out to be a street where significant relationships were formed for my family. It was the very street where my eldest brother, Manuel, met his future wife, who happened to live right across from our house. Little did I know at the time that same street would also lead me to a relationship that would profoundly affect my life.

She resided around the corner at the end of the street. My younger sister, Sandra, became close friends with her, and she would frequently spend time at our house. I found comfort in her presence, but being a naturally shy person, I constantly struggled to gather the courage to engage in conversation with her. Most of the time, my attempts were unsuccessful.

At the age of sixteen, I entered the workforce and purchased my very first car—a 1968 Chevy Camaro. It cost me a mere twenty-three hundred dollars. My father did not earn a substantial income; in fact, he lived from paycheck to paycheck and sometimes had to resort to loans just to cover our bills. Having emigrated from Mexico at a young age and with the unfortunate loss of both his parents shortly thereafter, he was forced to abandon his education and work on a farm back home. It was not until his wedding day that he finally met my mother, having connected through an advertisement in a Mexican newspaper. After their marriage, he secured a job at a steel factory in Michigan, where he spent thirty years operating a forklift before retiring. Our family seldom dined out except for the very occasional fast-food meal, and the only time we enjoyed a proper restaurant visit was when my dad received his income tax refund. Therefore, if we desired a car, we had to bear the financial burden ourselves.

At sixteen, I worked full-time and shouldered the cost of most of my expenses, including clothing. My mother worked part-time, but the majority of her earnings went toward paying bills, leaving her with very little discretionary income. Playing bingo brought her great joy, but due to financial constraints, she could not indulge in that pastime frequently. Recognizing her happiness derived from it, I made the decision to start paying rent, ensuring she had some extra money. Her gratitude was genuine and heartfelt. As a teenager, I had yet to fully comprehend the financial challenges associated with raising children, and my parents were faced with the responsibility of nurturing five of us.

At the age of sixteen, I found myself working full-time at a pizza shop, diligently crafting pizzas to cover the expenses of owning a car. It was during this time that I also started smoking pot, which eventually led to a challenging situation when I turned seventeen. Balancing forty hours of work with school became nearly impossible. School, in general, posed difficulties for me, particularly in spelling. The numerous rules and irregularities perplexed me, and I am so grateful for the convenience of spell-check today. As a student, I maintained an average grade of C, and looking back now, I could honestly admit that I struggled with a severe case of ADHD and possibly dyslexia. However, when it came to math, it came naturally to me. Numbers made sense, and it quickly became my favorite subject.

o   o   o

Knowing deep down that college was not in my future, I had a decision to make. I could either quit my job and give up my car or drop out of school. I chose the latter. You see, I did not mind hard work, and I enjoyed earning money to afford the things I needed and wanted. Besides, I was not ready to part with my car, and the idea of commuting to school by bus every day did not sit well with me.

Even though I left school, I still had a circle of friends from my former classmates and the neighborhood. They would often invite me to parties hosted by other students on the weekends. Sometimes I would drive, and other times it would be my friends. We always took turns.

When my friends were the ones driving, they would have to drop me off at the end of the night. I used this as an opportunity to potentially run into Kelly. As soon as my friend turned off the main road into our subdivision, I would ask them to pull over and let me out. When they questioned my request, I would simply say, "I need the exercise." The truth, however, was that I hoped to pass by Kelly's house for a chance to speak with her alone. This way, if she rejected me, at least no one else would witness it. As I mentioned before, I had always been shy around attractive girls, finding it nearly impossible to initiate or sustain a conversation. Yet with Kelly, it felt a bit easier since she had visited my house many times before.

After what felt like almost a year of passing by her house a couple of times a month, my persistence finally paid off. On a warm summer night, as I strolled down her street, I noticed she had just parked her striking Camaro Z28 in front of her house. The timing could not have been more perfect. As she stepped out of her car and caught sight of me walking by, she called out, "Danny, what are you doing walking in the middle of the street at this hour?"

I quickly thought on my feet and responded, "I went out with some friends, but since I live so close to the Main Street, they didn't want to drive me all the way home in a rush." Of course, I could not reveal the truth—that I had asked to be dropped off by the main road so I could casually walk past her house in the hopes of catching her outside. It would have come across as rather creepy.

She smiled and remarked, "That's pretty rude of your friends."

I nodded in agreement, saying, "I know, but it's only a couple of blocks away, so it's not a big deal." And just like that, we found ourselves engaged in a delightful conversation.

Around ten minutes into our chat, she rolled down the windows of her car and switched on the radio. I could vividly remember the first song that played that night—it was "Wheel in the Sky" by Journey. We continued standing in front of her house, engrossed in our discussion while enjoying the music. After an hour or so of sharing stories and moments, I mustered up the courage to ask her out. To my delight, she responded with a resounding yes! Her exact words were, "Yes, I would love to go out with you." A few more minutes passed, and she mentioned that it was getting late, hinting that she needed to go inside. I acknowledged the time and assured her that I would call her the next day.

o   o   o

Over the next couple of months, our relationship blossomed, and with each passing day, my feelings for her grew stronger. Around two months into our journey together, I managed to save up some money to take her out to a fancy restaurant. As we sat there, eagerly awaiting our food, she began asking me thought-provoking questions about my potential future. Hypothetically, she inquired how I envisioned myself ten years down the line. She wanted to know about the number of children I desired, the type of home I saw myself living in, and even whether I wanted a furry companion.

These questions caught me off guard since no one had ever delved into such discussions with me before. The idea of contemplating my life a mere two weeks ahead, let alone a decade, seemed foreign. As I pondered her questions, I mustered a response, saying, "I suppose I would like to have two or three kids." From there, I painted a picturesque image—a beautiful two-story house with a cozy fireplace in the master bedroom surrounded by a white picket fence and, yes, even a beloved dog.

Her face lit up with a radiant smile as I shared these aspirations, and when I finished, she exclaimed, "That's exactly how I picture my life too! I'm thrilled that we share the same dreams." As I gazed into her joyful eyes, a sense of happiness washed over me. It brought me immense joy to not only discover that she desired the same things in life but also realize that there was a possibility she wanted them alongside me.

After dropping her off that night, I returned home with an immense smile on my face—the kind of smile that emerges when you sense the stirrings of love. It was well past midnight when I entered my house, finding everyone sound asleep except for my brother Sam. Curious about my evening with Kelly, he inquired about it. I shared that we had an incredible time, revealing some details while keeping most of it to myself, wanting to savor the experience privately. Sam expressed his happiness for me and wished for things to work out.

○   ○   ○

A little while later, he proposed we smoke a joint together, and I agreed. By that time, I had been indulging in marijuana for a couple of years, often joining my brother for a smoke session several times a week. In fact, during that period, all our friends indulged in pot regularly—it was the fashionable thing to do. Ironically, I never found much enjoyment in it. Instead of experiencing the pleasure I assumed my friends did, it often induced feelings of paranoia in me. Countless times, I would find myself at a gathering, convinced that everyone was fixated on me, commenting on how stoned I appeared. It was far from a pleasant sensation. You might wonder why I continued to partake despite this; well, I did it because I did not want to be the odd one out among my friends. I did not want to be labeled as the square who abstained from smoking.

My brother and I decided to retreat to our room downstairs to smoke as our parents never detected the scent from there. After our session, I decided it was time for bed. Lying there, I reminisced about the incredible time I had with Kelly, how effortlessly our conversation flowed, and how we shared our hopes and dreams with each other.

However, after about ten minutes, reality struck, and my smile faded into a frown. I began contemplating the feasibility of the future I envisioned for myself, the one I had discussed with Kelly. Doubts crept in, whispering, "How will you ever achieve those aspirations? How can you accomplish all those things as a pizza maker and high school dropout?" Sleep eluded me that night as I looked at my life from a fresh perspective. I realized that there was no way I could fulfill the grand dreams we had shared, let alone provide Kelly with the life she desired, if I continued down my current path—a path where I was a pot-smoking pizza maker who had not finished high school. It dawned on me that if I wanted to make some of those dreams a reality, I had to chart a new course for my life, to diverge from the road I had been traveling.

o o o

In the following days, thoughts of how to accomplish the aspirations I had expressed consumed my mind. These desires were not just for Kelly's sake but for my own as well. I earnestly wanted to bring those dreams to life. I began contemplating various avenues for change, but a realization took hold deep within me—I understood that altering my life while remaining in the same social circle would yield little transformation. It became clear that to make substantial changes, I needed to distance myself from everyone, to embark on a complete overhaul. If I continued down the same path, surrounded by friends engaging in the behaviors I knew I needed to leave behind, it would be impossible to quit smoking pot and relinquish other detrimental habits.

Thus, about two weeks after our date, I made a life-altering decision. I headed to the local recruiting office and enlisted in the United States Army as a military police officer. This marked the beginning of a profound transformation.

I recognized that if I desired a different future, I had to change my present. Without altering my current circumstances, nothing about my future would truly change. Many of us can envision how we want our lives to look ten years from now, but we often fail to make changes in the present.

○   ○   ○

We need to remember that a lifetime is nothing more than a collection of individual days woven together. Moses has clearly grasped this concept. In Psalm 90 (NIV), if you read the initial verses, you will immediately sense his struggle with life. However, in verse 12 (NIV), he utters, "Teach us to number our days, that we may gain a heart of wisdom." Although I was not familiar with this verse or God at the time of my decision, I am grateful that he placed it in my heart.

The admonition to "teach us to number our days" urges us to recognize the significance of each day and ensure that we make each one count. It involves actively applying the principles and values that shape the desired trajectory of our lives to the choices and actions we take in the present moment. Though the concept may be straightforward, it encompasses a lifelong journey of intentional growth and alignment with God's will. By consistently investing in the study of his Word and integrating its wisdom into our daily lives, we lay the foundation for a more profound and meaningful relationship with God in the years to come.

Our lives unfold according to how we live each day. The same principle applies to our Christian journey and relationship with God. We can envision ourselves having a closer bond with him and a stronger faith a decade from now. Yet if our daily lives do not reflect that aspiration, our relationship with God will likely remain stagnant.

Consider Tiger Woods, for instance. We all know he was one of the world's greatest golfers. If you can somehow observe his everyday life as a teenager, you will understand that his actions have reflected the person he's become. He has sacrificed his teenage years on the golf course to become one of the greatest players. If we envision a closer relationship with God in ten years, we must ask ourselves, "Does my everyday life align with the kind of Christian I aspire to be? The only way to reach that desired relationship is by taking action today and doing what is necessary to get there. We must also acknowledge that it will require sacrifice—sacrifices of time and changes in our lives.

Seneca once said, "We are always complaining that our days are few, and acting as though there would be no end to them."

○   ○   ○

After completing three years in the military, two things became clear to me. Firstly, I realized that I did not want to become a police officer. I discovered there were a lot of politics as an officer, and the risks involved in the job outweighed the pay. I developed a deep respect for the men and women who put their lives on the line every day for the compensation they received. Secondly, I discovered that I wanted to escape the harsh winters of Michigan. Having traveled during my military service, I longed to live somewhere with milder winters.

Around a year after my discharge, an opportunity arose for me to work in Katy, Texas, and in 1985, I made the decision to pack up all my belongings and make the move. Being the first in my family to leave Michigan, it was not long before my entire family followed suit and settled in Katy. My father, who was born in Mexico but then moved to McAllen, Texas, when he was young, had initially planned to move back there after he retired. However, with all his children now residing in Katy, he chose to join us there instead.

○   ○   ○

Reflecting on my life, I consider joining the military to be one of the wisest decisions I have made. Although it has left me with some peculiar habits, such as my unwavering need to take a shower before doing anything else upon waking up in the morning (which used to frustrate my son when he was a young boy, especially on Christmas mornings) and my insistence on making my bed meticulously before leaving the room, I recognize the positive impact it has on me.

Despite feeling content with my relationship with God and believing I was on the right path, nothing truly changed in my walk with him. I continued living each day as I had before, engaging in activities that brought temporary pleasure like going out, getting drunk, and occasionally pursuing intimate encounters. The only adjustment I made was attending church sporadically, about two or three times a month. I convinced myself that as long as I showed up at church and did the right things, I was in good standing with God.

Until this point, I had not experienced salvation. Though I may have appeared as a follower of Christ outwardly, my inner being remained unclean. There were two crucial realizations that had yet to occur in my life. First, the light bulb of the Gospel, the good news, had not illuminated within me. Second, I had not genuinely repented from my sins. Later in this chapter, I would delve into what true repentance entails.

You see, during that time, my belief in the God of Christianity was distorted. It was a god of my own creation, designed to justify my own lifestyle. Unfortunately, many people today live in a similar manner. We often yearn for a God who firmly administers justice to those we deem worthy of judgment. However, when it comes to our own wrongdoings, we tend to hope that God turns a blind eye as we perceive our sins as inconsequential compared with those sensationalized in the media. We desire a God who is tolerant and accepting of who we are, seeking validation from others to affirm our choices.

o   o   o

I watched a video in which Oprah interviewed Joel Osteen. She posed the question "Do you think that gay people will go to heaven?" It would be important to note that she did not inquire about what the Bible said regarding the destiny of gay people. Instead, she sought Joel's affirmation of a particular lifestyle as if he possessed the authority to alter God's divine law. His response was, "Yes, I believe they will go to heaven," and that satisfied her. Additionally, it would be worth noting that Osteen did not provide any biblical verses to support his answer.

Sadly, many people today consider the opinion of a renowned figure to be the ultimate authority on matters of right and wrong.

It is essential for me to emphasize a clear truth: being heterosexual does not send someone into heaven, and being a morally upright person does not secure salvation. Regardless of one's sexual orientation or moral character, when a person comes to Christ and receives him as their Savior, a transformative change occurs on the inside that transforms their life. Basically, they start to alien their life into a Christlike life. Please grasp the profound reality that Jesus's purpose extends beyond our salvation; he has also come to bring healing and transformation to our way of living.

o   o   o

Over the next few years, I persisted in living life on my own terms without making significant changes. However, I held on to the belief that attending church intermittently would somehow keep me in God's favor.

One fateful day, a close friend extended an invitation for me to attend a men's Bible study class on a Saturday morning. The gathering took place at the same church my elder brother Manuel attended. I considered it a wise choice because I held great respect for Manuel's discernment in selecting a church with sound teaching.

You see, during Manuel's twenties, shortly after he and his wife had a baby boy, a couple of Jehovah's Witnesses knocked on his door. Intrigued by their words, he allowed them in, unaware of their teachings' inconsistencies with scripture. With limited knowledge of the Bible at the time, he found their conversation compelling. After about an hour, they invited him to one of their regular meetings, and he accepted the invitation.

That evening, Manuel shared his newfound belief with his wife, who inquired if he was certain about this path. He expressed his inclination toward their religion but resolved to attend one of their meetings to gather more information. His wife, supportive yet discerning, encouraged him to thoroughly investigate before making a significant decision. My brother possessed a remarkable quality: once committed to something, he pursued it wholeheartedly, immersing himself in books and resources until he grasped the subject inside out.

The following week, armed with his King James Bible, Manuel attended their meeting. About thirty minutes into the gathering, one of the teachers recited a passage from his Bible. Rising to his feet, my brother politely interrupted, stating, "My Bible doesn't say that."

Surprised, the instructor inquired about the version he used. Manuel replied, "I have a King James Bible."

The man responded, "That's the problem; you need a Jehovah's Bible for greater accuracy."

Perplexed and unsure of whom to believe, my brother returned home that night and confided in his wife, expressing his doubts. Determined to find the truth, he embarked on a journey of studying Hebrew and Greek, enrolling in college courses to learn how to read and write these ancient languages. His objective was to examine original manuscripts to verify the accuracy of his Bible translation. For an entire year, he delved into the depths of Hebrew and Greek, equipping himself with the tools necessary to scrutinize the scriptures.

Armed with copies of the original Old Testament writings, Manuel discovered that his Bible was indeed correct. Filled with confidence, he returned to the place where their meetings were held. Entering the class, he sought out the man who had urged him to acquire a new Bible. Displaying the evidence of the original writings and comparing it with his King James Bible, Manuel conclusively demonstrated the accuracy of his translation. In response, the man simply instructed him to leave and never return. This incident solidified my trust in Manuel's ability to discern a genuine and faithful church.

o   o   o

After attending my first Saturday morning Bible study class, I found myself deeply impressed. These men not only possessed a profound knowledge of scripture but also embodied the kind of character I aspired to emulate. It was not their worldly success that drew me to them; rather, it was their genuine desire to grow in Christlikeness. When the pastor opened the floor for prayer requests, these men did not seek material possessions or accolades. Instead, their petitions centered on seeking wisdom to become better husbands and fathers, aligning themselves with God's intended design for their lives. I observed that these men recognized their imperfections and, in humility, prayed for transformation to be more like Christ.

In just a few weeks of attending these enlightening Saturday morning sessions, I realized that my understanding of scripture had expanded more rapidly in just a few weeks than it had in the past year. This realization prompted a pivotal decision: I resolved to start attending the Sunday morning services as well. While my knowledge of scripture continued to grow, I understood that true transformation required more than intellectual insights. Although I still had much to learn compared with the seasoned members of the church, I sensed a deepening desire for personal change.

The church itself was relatively small, with about 120 members, and I found solace in its intimate atmosphere. The sense of belonging and familial connection was palpable among the congregation. Each person treated one another as family, fostering an environment conducive to spiritual growth and mutual support.

○　　○　　○

About a year and a half later, during a Sunday morning service, a profound revelation struck me. Pastor Buck was reading from the book of Matthew, where Jesus spoke about the contrasting paths to heaven and hell. The verses he read resonated deeply within me:

> Enter through the narrow gate. For wide is the gate and broad is the road that leads to destruction, and many enter through it. But small is the gate and narrow the road that leads to life, and only a few find it. (Matthew 7:13–14, NIV)

As soon as Pastor Buck concluded reading these words, an image flashed in my mind: a bustling eight-lane highway during rush hour with an off-ramp where cars were exiting the highway. It dawned on me that the eight lanes represented the wide road, the path to destruction, while the off-ramp symbolized the narrow road, the path to heaven. Contemplating this mental picture, a crucial question confronted me: What makes you believe you are on that off-ramp, the narrow road, simply because you attend church?

I began considering various people whom I deemed to be on the narrow road. My pastor, my trusted spiritual guide, undeniably belonged there as he exemplified a godly life distinct from most men I knew. J. Vernon McGee, an influential preacher, undoubtedly traveled that road, along with the esteemed Billy Graham. Furthermore, I thought about courageous missionaries who selflessly risked their lives to spread the Gospel in dangerous places. They, too, must be on that off-ramp.

I consider these two verses among the top three most alarming passages in the Bible, compelling every individual to pause and reflect. Jesus is unequivocally stating that the majority of people will end up on the path to destruction, with only a few discovering the way to eternal life. When we contemplate what Jesus is conveying, the contrast becomes stark—the road to hell is very wide, while the road to heaven is very narrow. To put it in perspective, let's attempt to quantify it with a percentage. Jesus said that one road is very wide, and the other is very narrow. What would you say the percentage of the narrow gate is compared to the wide gate? Ten percent? And, if we are going to be honest, that is being very conservative, I believe is more in the range of five percent. It is a sobering thought that should prompt us to examine ourselves.

Most people, however, read this verse without pausing to consider its gravity. They continue to read the verses that follow, perhaps interpreting them as if the road to heaven is about 40 percent—and the road to hell is 60 percent that still accommodating a significant number of people. It is essential to engage with these words at a deeper level, challenging ourselves to truly understand the gravity of the choices presented to us.

Yet amid these reflections, I could not escape the nagging question "What makes you think you are on that off-ramp? Is it merely because you attend church, possess a nice Bible, and dress well?" If that was the case, Jesus would have not referred it as a narrow road where only a few find it. At that moment, a profound realization gripped me—I understood that being in right standing with God required more than mere church attendance and outward goodness. For years, the world had fed me the notion that as long as I lived what I thought to be a morally upright life and refrained from harming others, I was deemed acceptable to God.

In another video I watched, Oprah engaged in a debate regarding the paths to heaven and hell. She expressed the belief that there are numerous roads that lead to heaven, implying that all religions offer a path to the same salvation. When a woman from the audience raised the question about Jesus, Oprah responded dismissively, suggesting that Jesus was just one among many ways to heaven. The woman countered by asserting that Jesus is the only way to heaven. In response, Oprah challenged her, asking, "Who are you to say that other religions cannot lead to heaven?"

However, what Oprah fails to comprehend is that it is not the woman herself making the claim that other religions are incapable of leading to heaven; it is Jesus himself who has declared it. We must grasp the truth that if all roads lead to heaven, then Christianity cannot be considered one of those roads.

In John 14:6 (NIV), Jesus himself proclaims, "I am the way and the truth and the life. No one comes to the Father except through me." This verse reveals a crucial understanding: Jesus is the exclusive path to the Father and eternal life.

We must confront a significant reality. If all roads lead to heaven, it forces us to consider two possibilities about God. Either he does not exist, making all religious beliefs irrelevant, or we are faced with a God who really does not care about our understanding of who he is. However, both options are highly unlikely. The truth is that the exclusivity of Jesus as the way to heaven highlights the significance of his divinity and the unique salvation he offers.

> They exchanged the truth of God for a lie, and worshiped
> and served created things rather than the Creator—who
> is forever praised. Amen. (Romans 1:25, NIV)

God deeply cares about our thoughts about him and how we approach him.

> For I can testify about them that they are zealous for
> God, but their zeal is not based on knowledge. (Romans
> 10:2, NIV)

Here it is emphasized that some people exhibit great zeal for God, but their zeal is not rooted in true knowledge and understanding. This verse highlights the importance of seeking genuine knowledge and insight about God to align our zeal with truth. It also emphasizes that our faith is not blind faith.

Furthermore, Psalm 145:18 (NIV) states, "The LORD is near to all who call on him, to all who call on him in truth." This assures us that the Lord is close to all who sincerely call on him, who approach him with truth and authenticity. This verse reminds us that God is intimately present with those who genuinely seek him and come before him in truth.

These passages emphasize the significance of pursuing a deep and genuine relationship with God, grounded in true knowledge and sincere devotion. God desires us to approach him with a sincere heart, seeking to know him more fully and to align our understanding of him with the truth revealed in his Word.

○   ○   ○

After the service, I approached Pastor Buck and asked if we could have lunch together. He kindly agreed, and we arranged to meet the next day. Over lunch, I shared with him how his sermon had deeply convicted me. I admitted that merely attending church did not guarantee my right standing with God. My pastor looked at me intently and affirmed that going to church alone does not make someone right with

God. He then quoted Ephesians 2:8 (NIV) to emphasize the importance of grace in our salvation:

> For it is by grace you have been saved, through faith—
> and this is not from yourselves, it is the gift of God—not
> by works, so that no one can boast.

He explained that our salvation is not something we can earn through our own efforts; it is a gift from God. He emphasized that when we sin, no number of good deeds can erase our wrongdoing. To illustrate this, he shared an analogy: Just as he could not persuade a judge to dismiss a ticket for speeding by promising to drive within the speed limit for a year, we could not erase our sins through good deeds. The ticket must be paid for the offense that was committed. Pastor Buck conveyed that the death of Jesus Christ on the cross serves as the payment for our sins—a gift available to all who accept it freely.

He further explained that although accepting God's gift of salvation is free, following Christ comes at a cost. It involves surrendering our old way of life and embracing a new life based on what Christ has done for us. To illustrate this, he quoted Matthew 10:39 (NIV):

> Whoever finds their life will lose it, and whoever loses
> their life for my sake will find it.

Jesus's words highlight that those who relinquish their own self-centered way of living and embrace the life God intended for us will find eternal life.

I like what C. S. Lewis once said: "Aim for heaven and you will get earth thrown in. Aim at earth and you get neither." This quote emphasizes the importance of prioritizing heavenly values and seeking a relationship with God above all else as it leads to a life that is truly fulfilling and meaningful.

Then Pastor Buck shared another relevant verse with me from the book of Luke that emphasizes the need to consider the cost of following Christ:

> And whoever does not carry their cross and follow me cannot be my disciple. Suppose one of you wants to build a tower. Won't you first sit down and estimate the cost to see if you have enough money to complete it? For if you lay the foundation and are not able to finish it, everyone who sees it will ridicule you, saying, "This person began to build and wasn't able to finish." (Luke 14:27–30, NIV)

During that conversation with my pastor, he emphasized the importance of understanding the potential sacrifices involved in wholeheartedly following Christ. He urged me to carefully consider the possible consequences of my decision. Choosing to be true followers of Christ may result in the loss of friendships with those who did not share our faith. It could even jeopardize my job security. However, my pastor assured me that there is one undeniable certainty: embracing a life of following Christ requires us to let go of our old ways. While in America the cost may not be significant, considering the potential loss of a friend or job, we must imagine the reality for believers in regions such as the Middle East or China, where the cost could be as extreme as their very lives. As his words resonated with me, I began to grasp the profound essence of being in right standing with God.

◦   ◦   ◦

I realized that being right with God meant acknowledging that I had been on the wrong path, recognizing my sinful nature, and not only confessing my sins but also surrendering my old life to live anew for him. It dawned on me that Jesus had done precisely this for us—he relinquished his heavenly life to come to the earth and ultimately died on the cross. I understood that God was not asking anything of us that he had not already done for our sake.

As these thoughts sank in, I felt a profound shift within me, grasping the significance of accepting God's gift of salvation and committing myself to a life dedicated to following Christ. It was a transformative realization that compelled me to make a decisive choice—to truly repent from my sins and to start walking a path of discipleship, even if it came at a cost. Now that I came to this point in my life where I truly understood what it meant to repent, let me share with you what that looks like.

Repentance involves a deep sorrow and a genuine turning away from sinful behavior, accompanied by a sincere desire to change and live in obedience to God. Repentance is not merely feeling sorry for one's actions but also taking the necessary steps to align one's life with God's will. This is what true repentance looks like:

Recognition of My Sin: Repentance begins with acknowledging and recognizing our sinful nature and actions. We realize that we have disobeyed God's commands and fallen short of his standards. This recognition leads to godly sorrow and conviction of our need for forgiveness.

> For all have sinned and fall short of the glory of God.
> (Romans 3:23, NIV)

Genuine Sorrow: True repentance involves sincere remorse and godly sorrow for our sins. This sorrow is not merely regretting the consequences of our actions but also understanding the offense it causes against God.

> Godly sorrow brings repentance that leads to salvation
> and leaves no regret, but worldly sorrow brings death.
> (2 Corinthians 7:10, NIV)

Confession: Repentance involves confessing our sins to God, acknowledging them openly and honestly before him. Confession demonstrates our humility and desire for forgiveness.

> If we confess our sins, he is faithful and just and will
> forgive us our sins and purify us from all unrighteousness.
> (1 John 1:9, NIV)

Turning Away: Repentance goes beyond remorse and confession; it requires a genuine turning away from sin. It involves a change of mind, heart, and direction, embracing a new way of life that aligns with God's commands. It involves changing the road we are on.

> Let the wicked forsake their ways and the unrighteous their thoughts. Let them turn to the LORD, and he will have mercy on them, and to our God, for he will freely pardon. (Isaiah 55:7, NIV)

God's Forgiveness and Restoration: When we genuinely repent, God graciously forgives our sins, cleanses us, and restores us to a right relationship with him. He extends his mercy, grace, and love to us.

If we confess our sins, he is faithful and just and will forgive us our sins and purify us from all unrighteousness. (1 John 1:9, NIV)

It is essential to grasp that becoming a believer and receiving God's grace does not imply immediate perfection or immunity from committing sins again. Let me illustrate this with an example that I learned from J. Vernon McGee. Two people, one a nonbeliever and the other a young believer, decide to unwind after work on a Friday night. They visit a few clubs and end up drinking excessively. As the night progresses, they meet women who express interest in going home with them. Both people end up taking the women to their respective places and engaging in sexual relationships.

The next morning, their responses to the previous night's actions differ greatly. The nonbeliever wakes up with excitement, thinking about how enjoyable the night has been and wanting to repeat it. However, the young believer wakes up with deep remorse and self-reflection. He realizes the mistake he has made and immediately falls to his knees, repenting to God.

This example illustrates the contrast between the mindset of someone who has not yet encountered God's grace and someone who has embraced faith but is still maturing in it. The believer's response, while not immune to sin, reveals a heart that acknowledges wrongdoing and seeks God's forgiveness.

○   ○   ○

In Christianity, receiving God's grace does not mean leading a perfect life or never sinning again. It means recognizing our imperfections, understanding our need for God's mercy, and actively seeking repentance and growth. The journey of faith involves continuous learning, transformation, and drawing closer to God, acknowledging that we are works in progress and dependent on his grace throughout our lives.

In summary, repentance involves recognizing our sin, experiencing godly sorrow, confessing our sins, turning away from sinful behavior, bearing fruit that reflects a changed life, and receiving God's forgiveness and restoration and his mercy and grace through his Son, Jesus. It is a transformative process that leads to a deeper relationship with God and a life lived in obedience to his will. This does not mean that we will start living a perfect life, by no means; we will continue to take two steps forward and one step back, but our hearts' desire should be to please him.

o   o   o

There will inevitably be moments in your journey where progress seems elusive, stretching into days, weeks, and even months. Certain sins may persist, taking years to gain control over, and you may find yourself questioning your salvation after countless perceived failures. During such trying times, remember the comforting words found in the book of Mark 16:6–7 (NIV).

On the Sabbath after Jesus's crucifixion, Mary Magdalene and Mary, the mother of James, arrived at the tomb with spices to anoint his body. To their astonishment, Jesus was not there. Instead, they encountered a man clothed in white who reassured them. "Don't be alarmed," he said. "You are looking for Jesus the Nazarene, who was crucified. He has risen! He is not here. See the place where they laid him. But go, tell his disciples and Peter, 'He is going ahead of you into Galilee. There you will see him, just as he told you.'"

Take note of the phrase *and Peter* in the angel's message. Despite Peter being one of the disciples, he is specifically singled out. Why?

Because Peter has recently denied Jesus three times, causing him immense remorse—similar to the way we beat ourselves up when we repeatedly fail. However, the scriptures also reveal that Peter genuinely loves Jesus, and that is what truly matters—our heart's disposition.

So in those moments when you feel overwhelmed by your shortcomings, remember the words "But go tell his disciples and [fill in your name here]." Even though Peter is a disciple, he is singly pointed out despite his failures; your love and devotion to God are what truly define your relationship with him. Do not allow repeated missteps to lead you astray. Instead, cling to the hope and knowledge that God's grace is abundant and his love is unconditional. Keep seeking his forgiveness, his guidance, and his transformative power, for he is faithful to complete the work he has begun in you.

Philippians 1:6 (NIV) being confident of this, that he who began a good work in you will carry it on to completion until the day of Christ Jesus.

○   ○   ○

That day was a turning point for me as I fully grasped the magnitude of what Christ had done for me. He sacrificially paid for my sins, offering me the opportunity to be reconciled with God and to spend eternity in his presence. It was a profound realization that stirred within me.

That night, humbled by this newfound understanding, I knelt down in prayer for the first time, not to a distorted image of God I had constructed in my mind but to the true God—the holy God revealed in the pages of the Bible. I approached him as the God of both wrath and love, recognizing his power to forgive through his Son.

In that moment, I recognized that God, as the Creator, knows what is truly best for us and how we ought to live. He alone possesses the wisdom to guide us toward a life filled with genuine joy—the joy of knowing that I have received forgiveness and that when I stand before him, I will be in good standing with him, not because of my own righteousness but because of the righteousness of Christ that has been imputed to me.

This revelation ignited a profound sense of gratitude and a desire to align my life with God's will. It marked the beginning of a journey where I sought to live in obedience to his teachings, trusting that his ways lead to true fulfillment and everlasting peace.

Let us see what Paul tells us in John 3:18–20 (NIV):

> Whoever believes in him is not condemned, but whoever does not believe stands condemned already because he has not believed in the name of God's one and only Son. This is the verdict: Light has come into the world, but men loved darkness instead of light because their deeds were evil. Everyone who does evil hates the light, and will not come into the light for fear that his deeds will be exposed.

It is worth considering that this reaction differs when we find ourselves in a doctor's office. In that context, we eagerly seek to uncover what is wrong so that we can address and rectify it. Similarly, the Word of God serves as a mirror, reflecting our true image. We may choose to ignore it, but it does not alter the reality that we are in need of Christ.

o   o   o

There was a memorable golf outing I had with my friend Arthur, an experience that remained etched in my memory. It all began when Arthur reached out to me, expressing his plans to visit Houston and asking if I could arrange a tee time for the following day. Without hesitation, I promptly organized a noon tee off on an unfamiliar course in Houston.

Arriving at the club at around eleven thirty, we hurriedly made our way to the clubhouse with only a brief interval before our tee time. Eager to warm up, we each grabbed a bucket of balls and headed toward the driving range. Because of the bustling atmosphere, we ended up occupying separate spots, with me securing the one closest to the clubhouse, while Arthur found a spot roughly ten slots away.

For some inexplicable reason, my drives were impeccably accurate that day, consistently sailing down the middle for about 275 yards. Bolstered by my confidence, I was convinced that I would outperform Arthur by a considerable margin. However, our focus was abruptly interrupted when we heard our names being called, signaling that we were up next to tee off on the first hole.

Observing Arthur making his way toward me, I positioned a ball on the tee and eagerly awaited his arrival. As he drew near, I could not contain my excitement and exclaimed, "Arthur, check this out!" With anticipation, I lined up my shot and struck the ball with precision, sending it soaring straight down the middle, matching my previous drives of about 275 yards.

Engrossed in watching my ball's trajectory, I held my swing position, with the club still resting over my shoulder. Unbeknownst to me, Arthur, too, was enjoying a successful round, eagerly selecting a ball from my bucket, and placing it on my tee to demonstrate his swing. As I turned around to face Arthur, my club inadvertently followed my motion, and to my dismay, the head of my driver collided forcefully with Arthur's mouth. The impact caused him to instinctively grab his injured mouth as he stumbled backward, clearly in pain.

As Arthur regained his balance and stood up, his eyes welled up with tears, and he appeared slightly disoriented. I immediately offered my sincere apologies multiple times, but Arthur understood that he should have never stepped into my swing, considering I had not completed it. Soon we noticed blood seeping through his fingers, prompting Arthur to swiftly retrieve his golf towel from his bag and press it against his injured mouth. Concerned for his well-being, I asked him if he was all right, to which he responded, "I think so, but man, did that hurt."

Curiosity and concern led me to request that Arthur remove the towel so I could assess the extent of the damage. As he unveiled the injury, it became apparent that I had split his upper lip all the way through, extending up to the bottom of his nose. Surprisingly, the bleeding had subsided, giving Arthur the impression that it was not too severe. However, upon witnessing the severity of the wound, I insisted, "Arthur, I need to take you to the hospital. You need stitches."

Ever the devoted golfer, Arthur glanced at me and affectionately called me Danielson, a nickname he had given me since our first meeting, and insisted that he merely needed something to hold his lip together, eager to continue playing. Despite my repeated pleas to prioritize his well-being, he stubbornly refused, maintaining his desire to proceed with the game. Determined to ensure his safety, I proposed, "Arthur, let's go into the bathroom and look in the mirror. If you still want to play after that, we can play."

His stubbornness persisted as he replied, "No, let's just play."

However, his resolve wavered when he noticed a woman from the clubhouse passing by. He approached her and inquired about the availability of butterfly stitches, but she regretfully informed him that they did not have any. However, she offered to bring him some Band-Aids instead, and Arthur told her, "Perfect, that would be great!"

O   O   O

As we patiently waited, a compassionate gentleman approached us, expressing concern for Arthur's well-being. Having witnessed the incident, he introduced himself as a doctor and offered to examine Arthur's lip. Relieved by the unexpected encounter, Arthur revealed his injured lip to the doctor, who declared, "Today is your lucky day. I just finished a round, and I am on my way to the hospital. Here is my card. Go to the hospital and ask for me to be paged, and I'll take good care of you right away." With those words, the doctor departed.

Excitedly, I exclaimed to Arthur, "That's great! Let's go." However, Arthur remained steadfast in his determination to play before seeking medical attention.

Eventually, I managed to persuade him to accompany me to the men's room, where he finally beheld his reflection in the mirror. Staring at his injured lip, he exclaimed, "Danielson, what on earth did you do to me? Why didn't you tell me it was this bad?" Finally acknowledging the severity of his condition, Arthur agreed to proceed to the hospital.

Once we arrived, we promptly paged the doctor, who promptly emerged and fulfilled his promise, attending to Arthur's injury just as he had assured. Remarkably, he provided his services free of charge, ensuring Arthur received the necessary care.

o   o   o

Regrettably, many people share a similar mindset to Arthur when it comes to approaching the Bible. They hesitate to delve into its teachings because they fear what it might reveal about their own sinful nature. The notion of being labeled as a sinner is unsettling for most people. They may acknowledge making mistakes along their journey but resist accepting the label of being a sinner.

I once hear pastor Timothy Keller eloquently express that when we gaze into the mirror of God's Word, two profound realizations unfold. Firstly, we come to recognize that we are a much bigger sinner than we have ever imagined. It unveils the depths of our flawed human nature and exposes the darkness within our hearts. This revelation can be uncomfortable and challenging to confront.

However, simultaneously, we also discover that we are loved far beyond what we've ever thought. Despite our inherent sinful nature and the mistakes we have made, God's love knows no bounds. It extends far beyond our comprehension and embraces us unconditionally. This realization of God's immense love offers hope, redemption, and the opportunity for transformation.

Just as Arthur eventually acknowledged the severity of his injury and sought the necessary care, we, too, must be willing to face the truth about our own imperfections and sinful tendencies. By doing so, we open ourselves up to the transformative power of God's love and the possibility of finding forgiveness, healing, and a renewed sense of purpose in our lives.

o   o   o

The second objection stems from the perception of exclusivity within Christianity. Ironically, there are other religions that also embrace exclusivity, yet such criticisms are rarely directed toward them. Furthermore, when compared with many other major religions, Christianity is arguably the least exclusive. Consider asking someone from another major religion if a murderer or a rapist or even if a gay person can enter the kingdom of heaven; the answer will be no. Surprisingly, there are numerous people in prison who have genuinely repented, turned to Christ, and experienced salvation.

I attended a church in Colorado Springs where we had a guest speaker from a prison whose warden allowed him to come and speak at our church. They presented a video showcasing his life behind bars, confined to a small cell. Remarkably, this man found profound joy in Jesus, surpassing that of many Christians outside prison, including myself. Witnessing this stirred joy in my heart and challenged the notion of exclusivity within Christianity.

o   o   o

Many years ago, I received news that one of my long-standing clients, whom I had been doing business with for a decade, was diagnosed with cancer and had about six months left to live. Upon learning this, I felt compelled to visit him and share the Gospel. While we had discussed God in the past, his belief was more centered on a deity he had crafted in his mind rather than the God depicted in scripture. I called his office to arrange a meeting, only to discover that, due to his condition, he was only present a couple of days a week. Thus, I scheduled an appointment for the following week.

When the day arrived, I met him at his office. He shared the details of his condition, describing the ups and downs he experienced. As I listened attentively, a silent prayer formed in my thoughts, asking God for an opportunity to share the Gospel with him. Then he revealed his awareness of having only a few months left to live, and I detected a tinge of fear in his voice. Seizing the moment, I asked him, "Jay, considering the limited time you have, have you ever pondered whether you are truly at peace with God?"

Pausing for a moment, he responded, "Yes, I believe I am OK, and I know I'll be going to a better place."

Curiosity piqued, I posed another question. "Jay, may I ask you something? How can you be certain that you are truly at peace with God? How do you know for sure?"

Reflecting, he said, "Daniel, I've been running this business for over two decades, and I've always conducted myself with integrity, prioritizing the best interests of my customers. In my two marriages, I've remained faithful, and I've strived to be a good father to my children."

Acknowledging his efforts, I replied, "Jay, it is commendable that you have endeavored to lead a virtuous life. However, according to the Bible, we cannot earn our way to heaven, no matter how morally upright we may be."

At this point, Jay's expression turned angry, and he retorted, "Look, I have lived a certain way for over sixty years, and I won't change that for anyone. This is who I am, and I believe I've done a pretty good job with my life."

Responding calmly, I said, "Jay, wouldn't you like to know what the Bible says about attaining eternal life? It is not merely a collection of stories; it is also a comprehensive narrative that begins with creation, explores how humanity rebelled against God, resulting in a separation between us and him. This separation necessitates a Savior, which is why God sent his Son to die on the cross, providing us with a means to reconcile with him and obtain eternal life."

Jay, still wearing a look of anger, exclaimed, "You can believe what you want, and I'll believe what I want. I've lived my life this way for over sixty years, and it works for me."

He continued, "I appreciate your intentions, but God knows I have not done anything deserving of hell. You have your beliefs, and I have mine. I will not change my lifestyle for anyone."

I responded, "All right, Jay. I just want you to know that you have been a loyal customer, and I appreciate that. If you ever have the desire to learn what the Bible truly says about eternal life, do not hesitate to call me. I will be there to discuss it with you."

In that moment, our conversation reached a standstill, leaving a sense of unresolved tension in the air. I departed, knowing that I had shared what was on my heart, knowing that I did my part as a follower of Christ.

Jay never reached out to me, and six months later, I found myself attending his funeral. The service was conducted by a priest who repeatedly assured everyone that Jay was now in a far superior realm. As I sat there, uncertain of whether Jay had embraced Christ before his passing, a recurring thought crossed my mind. It occurred to me that at every funeral I had attended, regardless of the person's spiritual condition, the sentiment of being in a better place was consistently expressed. It seemed that this statement was intended to provide solace and comfort to those present. However, it also created a false sense of assurance, perpetuating the belief that merely being a good person is sufficient to be in harmony with God, especially when it is coming from someone who seems to have an authority position in a church.

o   o   o

A few years later, I had a lunch date with a woman who had served in the military. During our conversation about God, she expressed her disbelief in Christianity, citing the notion that a good person could be condemned to hell by God. She found it difficult to reconcile the idea that a person's lack of belief in Christ could lead to eternal damnation. This is a struggle faced by many people.

In response, I explained to her that it is not God's decision to send someone to hell; rather, it is the person's own decision. She seemed puzzled and asked me to clarify. To illustrate my point, I shared an example from my son's life. I recounted how my sixteen-year-old son had gotten involved in graffiti with his friends. Concerned for his future, I sat him down and warned him about the consequences of continuing down that path, emphasizing that it could lead to a juvenile correction facility or even jail once he turned eighteen. Despite my repeated warnings, he chose not to heed my advice.

As expected, a year later, he was arrested for graffiti and spent thirty days in a correctional facility, just as I had forewarned him. I explained to her that my son is actually a good kid, and if she were to meet him, she would think highly of him. However, he had engaged in foolish actions. Then I posed a question to her. "Who was responsible for my son being sent to the correctional facility? Was it the judge or my son himself?"

She replied, "It was your son."

I affirmed her response and continued. On the day of his court hearing, my son asked me if I thought he would be sent to the correctional facility. I told him that I did not know, but if that were the outcome, it would be his own choosing. He looked at me, exclaiming, "This is not what I wanted! How can you say that to me? I do not want to go to detention."

I lovingly responded, "But I repeatedly warned you about the road you were on, and you did not take any action or listen to my counsel." I reassured him that despite the undesirable circumstances, my love for him remained unwavering.

I then proceeded to explain to her that the scriptures clearly indicate that we are all on the wrong path and need to make a change. However, if people choose to live their lives denying the existence of God and proclaiming self-sufficiency, believing they can thrive without him, then at the end of their lives, they will ultimately find themselves exactly where they desired to be—separated from God. This is what hell is: it is separation from God for all eternity.

She paused for a moment, contemplating my words, and then looked at me skeptically. With a hint of skepticism, she responded, "You trying to convince me that there is a God is like you trying to convince me that the color of grass is yellow." That was our last date.

o   o   o

Understanding and practicing patience is crucial when sharing the Gospel as it can be disheartening when, despite our efforts, some people remain resistant. One person who excels in defending the truth of the Bible is Frank Turek, a prominent apologist whose insightful discussions can be found on YouTube. During his debates, he employs a thought-provoking question. He pauses and asks his opponents, "If you discovered undeniable evidence that the Bible is true, would you become a Christian?" Their initial reaction is often confusion, prompting Turek to reiterate the question. "Imagine finding compelling evidence supporting the truth of the Bible. Would you become a Christian?" It astounds me how many people still respond with a firm no. C. S. Lewis once remarked that some people would rather face eternal damnation than bow the knee to Jesus. Ironically, the Bible assures us that every knee will eventually bow, whether it be during our encounter with God or when we stand before him.

> Therefore God exalted him to the highest place
> and gave him the name that is above every name,
> that at the name of Jesus every knee should bow,
> in heaven and on earth and under the earth,
> and every tongue acknowledge that Jesus Christ is Lord,
> to the glory of God the Father. (Philippians 2:9–11, NIV)

O   O   O

However, we should never give up on someone just because it seems like they will never believe. Many years ago, I embarked on a new job opportunity with a company based in Dallas while residing in Houston. It was during this time that I crossed paths with Arthur, and our friendship quickly grew. Golf became a shared passion, and every chance we had, we would engage in numerous rounds, squeezing in as much playtime as possible during my visits for meetings. Interestingly, our games were incredibly competitive, often coming down to the final hole to determine the victor. It puzzled me how we remained evenly matched despite Arthur's less-than-stellar swing off the tee. Regardless, we found joy in our friendly banter, always quick to rib each other whenever a shot veered off course, responding with, "Oh, what a shame … but thank you!"

Amid our golfing adventures, I would often seize the opportunity to share the Gospel with Arthur, especially during our extended hours on the golf course. Despite my efforts, he consistently rejected my words, swiftly changing the subject whenever religion entered the conversation. In one instance, he posed a question, seeking my opinion. Though the exact inquiry eluded me, I could distinctly remember offering a response based on God's perspective. His immediate retort struck a chord as he vehemently declared, "I do not care what God thinks. I want to know what you think." In that moment, I realized that Arthur probably would never receive Christ as his Savior.

○　　○　　○

Throughout our years with the company, Arthur and I also traveled together for conventions. The company assigned us shared hotel rooms, well aware of the strong bond we had formed. Unfortunately, on this particular outing, Arthur surrendered to temptation, engaging in infidelity and betraying his wife. Upon our return, I received an unexpected call from his wife the following morning. Aware of my Christian faith, she sought honesty as she posed the question "Did my husband cheat on me while the two of you were at this convention?"

Pausing momentarily, I responded, "What does your gut tell you?"

With conviction, she confided, "That he cheated."

I responded, "Go with your gut," and I hung up the phone. It was that moment that served as a pivotal trigger, hastening the inevitable end of their marriage.

The following day, I received a couple of calls from my coworkers expressing their disbelief at my actions toward my friend. One of them exclaimed, "I can't believe you would throw your friend under the bus like that."

I retorted, "Have you taken the time to confront him about what he did to his wife?"

To my surprise, he admitted, "No."

Seizing the opportunity, I posed a thought-provoking question. "Have you ever considered the possibility that Arthur could have contracted a life-threatening disease and then transmitted it to his wife?"

There was a momentary pause on the other end of the line, followed by an admission. "I never looked at it that way."

Seizing the opportunity for reflection, I gently suggested, "Perhaps it's worth contemplating." Eventually, he offered an apology for the hasty call.

To my surprise, Arthur never confronted me about the phone call I had with his wife, and on the surface, our friendship continued, but there was an underlying sense that things were not quite the same. Deep inside, I grappled with a dilemma—the challenge of maintaining a friendship with someone whose actions and choices contradicted my deeply held beliefs. It was a struggle as I wanted to be a source of positive influence in his life, but it seemed like an uphill battle.

In those moments of doubt, I could not help but reflect on my own past mistakes. Before I came to Christianity, I, too, had once succumbed to temptation and hurt someone close to me. However, by God's grace, I had experienced a transformation and witnessed how he had changed me for the better. This gave me hope that God could work in Arthur's life as well.

Despite my persistent efforts to share the Gospel with him throughout many years, it often felt as though my words were falling on deaf ears. I longed for him to experience the same life-changing encounter with God that I had, but it seemed like there were barriers he could not overcome.

Yet I held on to the belief that God's timing is perfect and that seeds of faith and love planted in a person's heart can take time to grow and flourish. So I continued to be a good friend to Arthur, hoping that through our interactions, he would one day see the depth of God's love and grace and make a transformative decision to follow him. I knew that sometimes our actions and consistent presence can speak louder than words, and I clung to the hope that my friendship with Arthur might be a testament to God's unfailing love and unyielding patience.

○   ○   ○

In time, we both took jobs with different companies and some distance was created between us while still maintaining our friendship. Years later, out of the blue, I received a call from Arthur while I was at work. He informed me that he was in Houston and asked if we could meet for lunch. I agreed, and as we sat down together, he began sharing something significant that had occurred in his life.

With a brief pause, Arthur confessed, "You know, Dan, I haven't been a good husband or father to my kids. My wife and I are divorced now, and there is not much I can do about that. However, I want to repair my relationship with my daughters, and I've been investing a lot of time in them."

He continued, "A few weeks ago, I went to church with my two girls, and during the service, the pastor spoke about reconciling with God. To make a long story short, I have surrendered my life to Christ."

Overjoyed, I expressed my happiness for Arthur's decision. I thanked him for reaching out and shared my appreciation for his openness. Arthur then confessed, "I also want to express my gratitude for all the things you shared with me about God throughout the years. Even though it may have seemed like I was not paying attention or did not care at the time, many of the things you said back then now make sense to me. So I wanted to let you know that it wasn't in vain."

Since that heartfelt conversation, Arthur and I have grown closer as friends. He has made significant positive changes in his life that are very evident to those who know him, and he is currently dating a Christian woman. I hope and pray that they will soon be getting married, and I am grateful for the transformative power of faith that has touched Arthur's life.

This is why I say never give up on people. God will surprise you.

o   o   o

Arthur also shared with me that day that due to all the things he had done in the past, he thought God would never forgive him. This misconception is a common mistake people make when deciding to surrender their lives to Christ. They believe that because of their past actions, God's forgiveness is unattainable. However, we must understand that Jesus's sacrificial death on the cross has paid for even the most heinous sins one can imagine. It covers all sins, not just minor ones.

Approaching Christ in our current state is akin to joining a gym without any prior fitness. It is not about waiting until we become perfect before coming to him; rather, it is about starting our journey with him as we are. Just as one does not wait to get in shape before beginning workouts, we do not need to wait to be spiritually fit before seeking Christ. One cannot become in shape without working out, and one cannot become spiritually fit without Christ. We must embark on our faith journey with him, knowing that through our relationship and commitment, we will be transformed and shaped into who he intends us to be.

Some people struggle with this concept because they think Jesus has only died for sins common to most people, excluding headline criminals like murderers and rapists. However, what Jesus has accomplished on the cross is not limited to specific sins; it encompasses all sins. It applies to anyone who approaches him with a genuine heart seeking forgiveness. A prime example of this is Saul, later known as Paul, who authored most of the New Testament. He was a man who would have made headlines today for his violent acts, including the persecution and killing of Christians. Yet once he turned from his destructive path and embraced the narrow road, God forgave him, transforming him into one of the most devout people in the Bible. That is why it is called *amazing grace!*

o   o   o

Many years ago I was talking to a friend who was going through some difficulties and the topic of God came up. He shared with me his experience of trying out Christianity and feeling like it did not work for him. He compared it to trying on a jacket that did not fit.

Unfortunately, there are instances where people misrepresent Christianity, leading others to believe that it guarantees a problem-free life. However, the narrow road of faith is not a path that magically resolves all our issues or makes life perfect. It is a challenging journey where new struggles arise. It involves going against the flow of the world, where the world is heading in one direction, while we strive to move in the opposite direction.

Let me share an example that illustrates this. When I was about nine years old, my mother took me, my two brothers, and their friend to Tiger Stadium to watch a baseball game. She dropped us off in front of the stadium and told us where she would pick us up later. As we entered the stadium, there was a vendor selling programs, and I asked my brother Sam if I could buy one with my own money. He agreed, saying he wanted to purchase one as well. I could not recall the exact amount I spent, but I cherished that program as if it were worth a million dollars.

Stepping into the seating area, even though we had upper-level seats due to financial constraints, I was awestruck when I saw the field. Words can hardly capture the overwhelming feeling, but anyone who has stood in the seating area of a baseball stadium as a child for the first time understands what I mean. Sometimes I ponder what it will be like walking into heaven, imagining the indescribable sensation.

As I sat there watching the Tigers players in their baseball uniforms, I thought that it was the best day of my life. Sharing the experience with my two elder brothers and one of their friends made it even more special.

After the exhilarating baseball game, we made our way down the ramps of the stadium to the designated meeting spot where our mother instructed us to gather. It felt like being part of a herd of cattle, and I tightly held on to the back of my brother Sam's shirt as we descended. About halfway down, a sudden realization struck me, and in a distressed voice, I exclaimed to Sam, "Sam, I left my program where we were sitting. We have to go back and get it."

Understanding my despair, Sam reassured me, "Don't worry, we'll go back. I just hope it's still there." Being a passionate sports fan himself, Sam empathized with the importance of that program. There was a time he shed tears when his beloved football team, the Minnesota Vikings, lost the Super Bowl when he was about thirteen years old.

Sam instructed me to hold tightly on to the back of his shirt as the four of us embarked on our journey back to our seats. It proved to be a challenging task as we moved against the stream of people descending the ramp. I observed Sam, my brother, and his friend skillfully maneuvering around people coming down the ramp. This is an example of what it can look like when choosing the narrow road, where we go in the opposite direction of the crowd. Thankfully, since I was behind my brother, the journey was somewhat easier for me, and the three of them walking together made it more manageable for them. This illustrates the importance of walking our Christian path alongside fellow believers; it is not a road we should attempt to navigate alone.

Upon reaching our seats, we discovered that my program was missing. Someone had taken it. Witnessing my disappointment, my brother Sam kindly handed me his program and insisted that I keep it.

The narrow road to heaven does not promise an easy life or the resolution of all our problems. On the contrary, it assures us that the journey will be challenging.

o   o   o

Let us take a closer look at who Paul was before his encounter on the road to Damascus, where he met Jesus and experienced a profound transformation. He held a position of authority as a government official, serving in the Sanhedrin. Paul not only was well educated but also enjoyed material wealth. He commanded respect from others, and he possessed official documents that granted him the power to persecute and even execute those whom he deemed followers of Christ. However, everything changed when he encountered Christ.

In that life-altering moment, Paul abandoned his former identity and embraced humility, recognizing his own sins and shortcomings. This pivotal event marked the beginning of his journey of transformation. He willingly let go of his old life and wholeheartedly committed himself to a new life aligned with God's purpose and teachings. Paul's path diverged from the wide road of popularity and power as he wholeheartedly embraced the narrow road of servanthood to God.

The radical shift in Paul's life reflects the power of encountering Christ and the transformative impact it can have on a person. His example serves as a reminder that no matter our past accomplishments, positions, or possessions, we all need to humbly acknowledge our flaws and turn to God for forgiveness and guidance. Paul's journey from persecutor to servant exemplifies the potential for profound personal change and the transformative power of God's grace.

So Paul's decision to follow this path did not lead to an easier life. On the contrary, his journey on the narrow road brought him greater challenges and struggles. With each step he took, the difficulties intensified, and the obstacles multiplied.

Here are some examples of what Paul went through as a follower of Christ. Second Corinthians 11: 23–29 (NIV) shows Paul's life after meeting Jesus:

> I have worked much harder, been in prison more frequently, been flogged more severely, and been exposed to death again and again. Five times I received from the Jews the forty lashes minus one. Three times I was beaten with rods, once I was stoned, three times I was shipwrecked, I spent a night and a day in the open sea, I have been constantly on the move. I have been in danger from rivers, in danger from bandits, in danger from my own countrymen, in danger from Gentiles; in danger in the city, in danger in the country, in danger at sea; and in danger from false brothers. I have labored and toiled and have often gone without sleep; I have known hunger and thirst and have often gone without food; I have been cold and naked. Besides everything else, I face daily the pressure of my concern for all the churches. Who is weak, and I do not feel weak? Who is led into sin, and I do not inwardly burn?

Despite enduring unimaginable hardships, Paul demonstrated remarkable resilience and determination. It is awe inspiring that amid his trials, he was able to write a significant portion of the New Testament. The source of Paul's enduring hope and joy in the midst of suffering could be attributed to the profound truth he embraced—the truth of what awaited him at the end of the narrow road.

○   ○   ○

Paul was fully aware of his imperfections, understanding that the narrow road would be fraught with difficulties. However, he refused to dwell on his past mistakes or his current position on the road. Instead, Paul fixated his gaze on the ultimate rewards that awaited him at the journey's end. He found purpose in his life while traversing the narrow road, keeping his focus on the eternal significance of his mission and the glorious destination that awaited him.

Paul writes in Philippians 3:12–14 (NIV):

> Not that I have already obtained all this, or have already arrived at my goal, but I press on to take hold of that for which Christ Jesus took hold of me. Brothers and sisters, I do not consider myself yet to have taken hold of it. But one thing I do: Forgetting what is behind and straining toward what is ahead, I press on toward the goal to win the prize for which God has called me heavenward in Christ Jesus.

Paul writes in 2 Corinthians 4:17–18 (NIV):

> Therefore we do not lose heart. Though outwardly we are wasting away, yet inwardly we are being renewed day by day. For our light and momentary troubles are achieving for us an eternal glory that far outweighs them all. So we fix our eyes not on what is seen, but on what is unseen, since what is seen is temporary, but what is unseen is eternal.

○   ○   ○

When I've embarked on this narrow road, it appears to defy the norms of this world. It seems as though God's Word is turned upside down, but in reality, it is humanity that has distorted God's original intentions. This road has taught me a profound lesson: if I desire to be first, I must first embrace the posture of being last and of humility and servanthood.

In Mark 9:33–35 (NIV), it says:

> They came to Capernaum. When he was in the house, he asked them, "What were you arguing about on the road?" But they kept quiet because on the way they had argued about who was the greatest.
>
> Sitting down, Jesus called the Twelve and said, "Anyone who wants to be first must be the very last, and the servant of all."

It is a road that reminds me that if I exalt myself, I will be humbled, but if I humble myself, I will be exalted.

> To some who were confident of their own righteousness and looked down on everyone else, Jesus told this parable: "Two men went up to the temple to pray, one a Pharisee and the other a tax collector. The Pharisee stood by himself and prayed: 'God, I thank you that I am not like other people—robbers, evildoers, adulterers— or even like this tax collector. I fast twice a week and give a tenth of all I get.'
>
> "But the tax collector stood at a distance. He would not even look up to heaven, but beat his breast and said, 'God, have mercy on me, a sinner.'
>
> "I tell you that this man, rather than the other, went home justified before God. For all those who exalt themselves will be humbled, and those who humble themselves will be exalted." (Luke 18:9–14, NIV)

○   ○   ○

These teachings on the narrow road reveal profound truths about the Christian journey. As we walk this path, it calls us to embrace humility, selflessness, and a heart of servanthood. Such values and priorities may differ significantly from those promoted by the world around us. Yet despite the challenges and opposition we may encounter, this road is undeniably worth pursuing as it leads us closer to God and aligns us with his divine kingdom. It is a road that challenges us to do the opposite of what our human nature wants to do.

It is essential to clarify that embodying these qualities of humility and selflessness does not imply that one cannot attain wealth or prosperity. Instead, the transformation lies in the way one views and utilizes their wealth. Understanding that their abundance is not solely about self-indulgence but about aiding those in need, people with this perspective exemplify the nature of Jesus's teachings. In acknowledging that there will always be people in need, we have the opportunity to reflect the compassionate nature of Christ by extending a helping hand to those less fortunate. This selfless approach to wealth aligns with Christ's teachings and fosters a heart of generosity, allowing us to become instruments of God's love and compassion in the world.

> You have heard that it was said, "Love your neighbor and hate your enemy." But I tell you: Love your enemies and pray for those who persecute you, that you may be sons of your Father in heaven. He causes his sun to rise on the evil and the good, and sends rain on the righteous and the unrighteous. If you love those who love you, what reward will you get? Are not even the tax collectors doing that? And if you greet only your brothers, what are you doing more than others? Do not even pagans do that? (Matthew 5:43–47, NIV)

Here, Jesus challenges the conventional understanding of love and expands the concept to include loving one's enemies. He starts by referencing a common teaching of that time (and is still used today), which is to love your neighbor but hate your enemy. However, Jesus introduces a radical shift in perspective by instructing his followers to love even those who are their enemies and to pray for those who persecute them.

o   o   o

By loving our enemies, Jesus explains that we demonstrate a characteristic of being children of God. God's love is not limited or selective but extends to both the righteous and the unrighteous. He illustrates this by pointing out that God causes the sun to rise and the rain to fall on everyone, regardless of their moral standing.

Jesus challenges his listeners further by asking what reward there is in loving only those who love them back. Even tax collectors, who have been considered social outcasts, have shown love to those who love them. Jesus urges his followers to go beyond societal norms and expectations, highlighting that simply greeting or showing kindness to their own group (brothers) is not a remarkable action because even pagans do the same.

The essence of Jesus's teaching is that, as followers of Christ, we are called to be different from the world, to be held to a higher standard of love and compassion. We are to love not only those who are easy to love but also those who oppose or mistreat us. Through this radical love, we reflect the character of our heavenly Father and demonstrate the transformative power of God's love in our lives.

Martin Luther King, Jr. grasped this principle with exceptional clarity. He recognized that the antidote to hate is, in fact, love. Jesus imparts these radical perspectives not to complicate our lives but to transform the world itself.

While I understand the challenges of this road, I recognize that my struggles pale in comparison to the persecution endured by Christians in other parts of the world, where faith can cost them their lives. As I am writing this, I have decided to do some research, and to my amazement, I've discovered that there are about one hundred million Christians all over the world today who are being persecuted. However, I believe that these favorable times in our own country may be drawing to a close. I believe that there are stages that are being set in place for Christians to be persecuted soon. Despite all this, there is one thing that continues to motivate me: I know where this road leads and the ultimate reward that awaits at its end.

o   o   o

In the TV series *Friday Night Lights*, during the halftime of the state championship game, the head coach delivered a powerful message. Though I could not recall the exact score, the team was significantly behind. As the coach entered the locker room, he said to his players, "Every man, at some point in his life, is going to lose a battle. He will fight and he is going to lose. But what defines him as a man is that, amidst the battle, he does not lose himself. This battle is not over."

I find great inspiration in those words. Similarly, our Christian walk is often filled with obstacles, moments when we find ourselves knocked down. Though there may be times when I feel like I have failed, I can always turn to scripture. It is in those moments that I find strength and remember my identity and purpose in life, preventing me from losing myself.

Understanding the challenges and the potential hardships that lie ahead, I am reminded of the perseverance, resilience, and faith that define our journey. While the road may be arduous, the knowledge of the destination and the assurance of God's promises keep me steadfast. With scripture as my guide, I press on, knowing that my identity and purpose are rooted in Christ.

As I confront the inevitable challenges and potential hardships that lie ahead, I find solace in the assurance of God's promise of peace throughout my journey. Though the path may be demanding and trying, the certainty of the destination and the unwavering faith in God's promises anchor me in unwavering resolve. The peace that God offers transcends the difficulties I may encounter; it is a profound peace rooted in the knowledge that when I stand before him, I will not be condemned for my sins.

Often, we overlook opportunities for profound growth when faced with life's challenges. In our earnest attempts to relieve our difficulties, we neglect a crucial step – pausing to inquire of God what He seeks to teach us.

In the movie "Return to Me," a woman falls in love with a man, only to discover a unique twist. Having undergone a heart transplant, she learns that the heart donor was the man's deceased wife. Overwhelmed with confusion and tears, she asks God, "What were you thinking?" In response, her grandfather offers a profound perspective, he walks up to her, holds up her face and says "It is the character that is the strongest that God gives the most challenges," and then adds, "Take that as a compliment."

When adversity strikes, take a moment to pause and ask God to reveal the lessons within. You might be pleasantly surprised by the insights gained when you allow yourself the time to grow.

O   O   O

Daniel Webster, who served as the secretary of state to two presidents, was once asked about the greatest thought occupying a person's mind. Without hesitation, he responded, "It is their accountability to God." This accountability brings a profound peace—a peace that arises from being right with God. It is a joyous assurance of our eternal destination, knowing that when we stand before God, Christ himself will testify on our behalf. True peace does not eliminate the challenges that arise in our lives; rather, it stems from a deep understanding and acknowledgment that God exists and that he is more than sufficient in every aspect of our lives. That is why Jesus says in John 16:33 (NIV):

> I have told you these things, so that in me you may have peace. In this world you will have trouble. But take heart! I have overcome the world.

> In essence, the peace that God promises is not a mere absence of difficulties but a profound recognition that he is present and fully capable of carrying us through every trial. It is a peace that surpasses understanding and sustains us in times of turmoil. With this peace, we

can confidently navigate the trials of life, knowing that our accountability to God is secure and that our eternal destiny is secure in his hands.

In addition to everything mentioned, it brings me comfort to know that when I stumble and fall along this narrow road, it is OK. I understand that it is through these struggles that God shapes me into the person he intends me to be. The difficulties and challenges I encounter along the way serve to strengthen my faith and deepen my relationship with God.

As stated in Romans 5:1–5 (NIV):

> Therefore, since we have been justified through faith, we have peace with God through our Lord Jesus Christ, through whom we have gained access by faith into this grace in which we now stand. And we boast in the hope of the glory of God. Not only so, but we also glory in our sufferings, because we know that suffering produces perseverance; perseverance, character; and character, hope. And hope does not put us to shame, because God's love has been poured out into our hearts through the Holy Spirit, who has been given to us.

Furthermore, not only does God utilizes my struggles and difficulties for my growth but he also promises to work all things, including failures and challenges, for the good of those who love him. As Romans 8:28 assures, God's purposeful work extends to every aspect of my life. Knowing this, I can find encouragement and trust that even in the midst of hardships, God is at work, guiding me along the narrow road and bringing about his good and perfect plan.

o o o

Even in the midst of Paul's imprisonment, shackled to a Roman guard day and night, Paul exemplified a remarkable spirit of joy. From his confinement, he penned a letter to the Philippians, known today as the book of Philippians, sharing his insights on attaining true joy. Paul's ability to rejoice stemmed from his unwavering knowledge of his identity as a child of God and his conviction that he was precisely where God intended him to be. He refused to allow his circumstances dictate his inner state. Instead, he found joy in the sufficiency of Christ and shifted his focus from his situation to his divine calling. It was this focus on fulfilling God's purpose for his life that brought him lasting joy, even in the confines of prison. Remarkably, even while incarcerated, Paul continued to proclaim the Gospel, and his unwavering faith had a profound impact. His unwavering commitment to the Gospel spread throughout the palace, even to Caesar's Roman guards themselves.

In the book of Philippians, specifically in chapter 1 verses 12–14, Paul affirms his perspective.

> Now I want you to know, brothers and sisters, that what has happened to me has actually served to advance the gospel. As a result, it has become clear throughout the whole palace guard and to everyone else that I am in chains for Christ. And because of my chains, most of the brothers and sisters have become confident in the Lord and dare all the more to proclaim the gospel without fear. (Philippians 1:12–14, NIV)

Paul's unwavering joy in the face of adversity serves as a powerful reminder that our circumstances do not have to define our outlook. By anchoring ourselves in our identity as children of God and embracing his calling on our lives, we, too, can experience a profound sense of joy, regardless of the challenges we may face. Like Paul, may we find strength in Christ and boldly fulfill our purpose, trusting that even in the midst of trials, the message of the Gospel can bring encouragement, courage, and transformation to those around us.

O   O   O

Throughout our journey, there may be moments where we stumble and experience failures along the way. It is natural to question ourselves, wondering if we are truly in right standing with God. However, it is important to recognize that it is perfectly normal to have these doubts and concerns. In fact, it is a sign of genuine faith and a desire to grow closer to God.

Those who are not OK with God rarely question their relationship with him. So if we find ourselves asking these introspective questions, it shows that we are seeking a deeper connection with our Creator. The key lies in examining our hearts. Do we feel remorse when we fall short? Are we earnestly striving to please him despite our setbacks?

If the answer to these questions is yes, then we can take solace in knowing that we are indeed in good standing with God. Our genuine remorse and continuous effort to please him demonstrate our sincerity and commitment. God understands our human nature and the challenges we face. If we sincerely love and seek him and repent when we stumble, striving to align our lives with his will, we can find assurance that we are on the right path.

So in moments of doubt and questioning, remember that it is the presence of these concerns that affirms your genuine desire to be in good standing with God. Trust in his grace, seek his forgiveness, and continue to press forward on the narrow road with faith and perseverance.

As for Kelly, the girl around the corner of my street, you may be curious about what happened to her. Well, six months after my deployment, I received a Dear John from her. Interestingly, I discovered that several of my buddies had also received similar letters during our first year in the military. It was not something I held against her; I did not expect a young girl to wait for years while I embarked on my military journey.

Life has a way of taking unexpected turns, and it was evident that our paths were meant to diverge at that point. While it was disappointing, I understood that circumstances and personal growth often lead people in different directions. The challenges and sacrifices of military life can put a strain on relationships, especially for those waiting at home.

Though our paths went separate ways, I held no resentment toward Kelly. I recognized the reality of the situation and understood that it was a decision made based on her own life circumstances and aspirations. People change, circumstances change, and sometimes relationships need to evolve accordingly.

In the grand scheme of things, it is a valuable lesson about the complexities of life and the need to adapt to unforeseen circumstances. It serves as a reminder that our journeys are filled with twists and turns, and sometimes we must let go of certain expectations and embrace the new paths that unfold before us.

As time went on, I focused on my military service, personal growth, and the connections I made along the way. Each experience played a part in shaping me into the person I am today. Life moved forward, and so did I, carrying the memories and lessons learned from that chapter of my life with a sense of understanding and gratitude.

CHAPTER 3

RELATIONSHIPS

When it comes to relationships, if I am going to be honest with myself, I must admit that I have not had much success. I have been through two divorces, and now I find myself in my third marriage. However, I want to emphasize that in the past, I was not the Christian man that I am today. In my first marriage, I was not a follower of Christ, and neither one of us treated each other with the love and respect that God intended for a husband and wife. Now I do not believe that one must be a Christian to make a marriage last, but as a Christian today, divorce is not something I believe in, and my current wife shares the same belief.

My first wife became pregnant shortly after our marriage, and within a year after our son was born, we got a divorce; both of us were to blame. As for my second marriage, it was a chapter I preferred not to dwell on because it was even shorter, lasting about six months. Despite being a devoted Christian at the time of my second marriage, I was still very young in my faith journey and lacked maturity in my relationship with God. I was in no position to seek a godly wife or build a marriage founded on scriptural principles.

I share these experiences not to dwell on the past but to acknowledge my past shortcomings as a young Christian. Through these failures, I have learned the importance of building relationships on faith and mutual respect. Today I strive to apply those lessons and nurture a healthy, God-honoring marriage with my current wife. However, I am far from perfect with my share of flaws (just ask my wife), yet I strive to improve each year to honor the One who created me—God.

○   ○   ○

It truly is a wonder that I've even managed to get married, let alone three times. You see, I have always struggled with shyness, especially when it comes to engaging in conversations with women I am attracted to. Whenever I happen to encounter an attractive woman, my nerves will get the best of me. I will freeze up, unable to find the right words to start a conversation. Sometimes a woman will even make it easier for me by offering a smile as she walks by me in a store, but that only intensifies my struggle. I will desperately try to think of the perfect thing to say, but my mind will become overwhelmed with various lines, each sounding corny or even desperate upon reflection.

So there I will stand, pretending to be engrossed in an item of interest while inwardly grappling with the pressure to come up with the ideal conversation starter. Deep down, I know that once the conversation begins, I can relax a little, but the challenge is finding those initial words. This torturous cycle will persist for a while, and then all of sudden, it will hit me—the perfect thing to say, especially given the store we are in or the circumstances surrounding the encounter, unfortunately comes to me about thirty minutes later while I am in my car on the way home.

It is frustrating to realize that the ideal words come to me only when it is too late, long after the opportunity has passed. Yet despite these struggles, I believe that God works in mysterious ways, guiding me through the challenges of relationships and teaching me important lessons along the way. And despite my shyness and missed opportunities,

I am grateful that I have found someone who shares the same beliefs that I do.

○ ○ ○

You see, one of the most challenging things for me as a man is facing rejection from a woman, especially when others are present. It feels like everyone within a fifty-foot radius is watching and waiting to see if I will be rejected. As I reflect on this issue, I can trace its origins back to sixth grade.

My teacher Mrs. Kennedy was one of my favorites. Mrs. Kennedy taught both fifth and sixth graders in the same class—an impressive feat. Among my classmates was a girl named Amy, who, despite being in the fifth grade, was the cutest girl I had ever encountered at that point in my young life. I genuinely looked forward to going to school each day, simply knowing that she would be there. Occasionally, our teacher would assign group projects, dividing us into groups of three or four. Whenever Amy and I were placed in the same group, I became ecstatic. Those moments working together on projects were some of the happiest days of sixth grade.

Now there were only two people who knew about my crush on Amy, although they were not aware of the depth of my feelings. One of them was my good friend in class, Matt, who was quite understanding about it and even found himself having a similar crush. The other person was my elder brother Sam, and confiding in him turned out to be a big mistake.

On a winter Saturday afternoon, my brothers and several neighborhood kids gathered to play football in the snowy field near our house. While we were engrossed in the game, Amy and her sister, who lived a couple of blocks away, happened to walk across the field on their way to the drugstore located on the other side. It was a common practice back then for our parents to send us to the store whenever they needed something, and cutting through the field was easier than driving around the block, even in the winter.

After Amy and her sister passed by where we were playing, my brother caught me stealing glances in her direction. He asked me, "Isn't that Amy?"

I acted as if I had not heard him, but he persisted, saying, "Danny, isn't that Amy, the girl you like?"

With a cautious voice, I replied, "I think so. I'm not sure," all the while knowing deep down that it was indeed her from the moment she set foot on the field.

I did not want to make a big deal out of it, so I kept thinking, *Please do not say anything to embarrass me.* Thankfully, he refrained from doing so.

However, I knew that as they walked to the store, they would eventually have to cross back through the field to return home. Sure enough, about fifteen minutes later, they were making their way back. As they passed by the field where we were playing, my brother suddenly yelled out with a loud voice, "Amy!"

In a panic, I pleaded, "Sam, what are you doing? Please don't say anything."

But the more I tried to stop him, the more determined he seemed to be in getting her attention. Once again, he shouted "Amy!"

This time, Amy and her sister halted their steps, both turning to look in our direction. And then to my utter devastation, Sam blurted out, "My brother likes you and wants to know if you will go with him."

I was crushed. I could not believe my brother had just exposed my feelings like that. Back in elementary school, you did not ask a girl out or propose going steady. Instead, you would simply ask her if she would "go with me," and if she said yes, it meant we were now a couple.

o   o   o

After my brother had humiliated me in front of everyone, I mustered the courage to confront him, asking, "Why did you do that?"

He responded, "Do you like her, or don't you?"

I hesitated and then admitted, "Yeah."

"Well, now you'll know if she likes you."

Devastated by his actions, I no longer felt like playing football. All I wanted was to go home.

Later that night, lying in bed across from my brother, I asked him, "Sam, why did you have to do that?"

Posing as if he did not understand, he replied, "Do what?"

Feeling frustrated, I said, "You know, say what you said to Amy."

In response, he simply asked, "What's the worst that can happen? She says no. But what if she says yes?"

Lying there in bed, those words echoed in my mind. What if she did say yes? However, the thought of her saying yes seemed unimaginable. She was so cute that I could not fathom her accepting my proposal. Despite being friends, I could not envision her becoming my girlfriend. For some reason, even though she was in the fifth grade and I was in the sixth grade, I felt as though she was out of my league.

O   O   O

The next morning, filled with nervousness about facing Amy at school, I devised a plan—I would pretend to be sick. I stayed in bed, feigning illness, hoping to avoid the encounter. However, my ruse did not last long. My mother noticed my prolonged absence and came upstairs, questioning, "Why are you still in bed? Didn't your brother wake you up before he left for school?"

Trying to convince her, I weakly replied, "Yes, but I don't feel good."

My mother, perceptive as ever, placed her hand on my forehead and declared, "You're not sick. Get up; get dressed. You are going to school." I attempted to prolong my stay, hoping she would change her mind, but she insisted I get ready.

Reluctantly, I got dressed, hoping for a last-minute reprieve. As I descended the stairs to the living room, my mother instructed, "Hurry up, put on your boots and jacket. I'm giving you a ride."

I found myself seated in the back seat of her car, on my way to school. Anxiety consumed me as I contemplated facing Amy. Desperate for an escape, I made one last attempt, saying to my mother in a sickly voice, "Mom, I really don't feel well. Can I just go back to bed?"

Her response was firm. "Once you are in class, you'll start feeling better. I don't want to hear any more about it."

With each passing moment on the way to school, my nerves heightened. My only hope was that Amy would be absent due to illness. In prayer, I pleaded, *Oh please, God, let her be sick today.*

After my mother dropped me off, I entered the school with a sense of dread. Making my way to the coatrack on the left wall, where we hung our jackets and left our boots, I stole a quick glance to the right, hoping to catch sight of Amy's desk. To my astonishment, her desk was empty. Could it be that my prayer had been answered and she was not attending school that day? As I removed my jacket, I double-checked, and indeed, all the other kids were at their desks except Amy. A surge of relief washed over me as if a heavy burden had been lifted. I sat down on the floor to remove my boots, those over-the-shoe kind with the large buckle snaps that required both hands to remove.

While working on my left boot, I noticed someone passing by from my peripheral vision. Curiosity got the better of me, and I looked up. To my disbelief, it was Amy hanging up her jacket. My heart sank, and I continued to slowly remove my boot, keeping my head down, hoping she would pass without saying a word. Pretending not to notice her, I saw, from the corner of my eye, as she walked toward her desk, but just as I was starting to feel a glimmer of hope, she stopped about five feet away from me, turned around, and walked back toward me. With a solemn expression, she uttered, "Hey, Danny, I heard what your brother said, and the answer is absolutely not!" Absolutely not—can you believe that? No wonder why I am so shy with pretty girls.

o   o   o

Many years later, I crossed paths with my first wife. We met in a club, and I'd understand what you might be thinking. However, during that time, many of the people I knew met their spouses in similar venues. We hit it off immediately, and within a year, we were engaged.

Instead of waiting until after the wedding to live together, we decided to get an apartment while still engaged. It seemed like a common practice among the people we knew.

Throughout the years, I bought into those old sayings like "No one buys a pair of shoes before trying them on or purchases a car before taking it for a test-drive." Looking back now, I realized how foolish it was to apply those comparisons to someone who was about to become my wife. It did not make any sense at all.

Our culture has deeply ingrained the belief that sex must happen before marriage. In fact, if you are to announce today that you are choosing to abstain from sex until marriage, you may even be subjected to mockery. We are heavily influenced by a culture that often dismisses or distorts the concept of God. If they do acknowledge a higher power, it is often a god created by society or the universe rather than the God portrayed in the scriptures. We are being molded by a culture that thinks it knows what is best for us, even if it costs us our eternal soul.

O   O   O

Before delving more into controversial topics such as God's moral law, it is crucial to awaken ourselves to an essential truth about the world we inhabit, irrespective of the century we are in. We must understand that if there truly is a God (which there is), it is only logical that his moral law, given the diverse cultures worldwide, will inevitably include laws that may offend certain cultures while not affecting others. Similarly, there will be different laws that offend different cultures.

It is important to realize that encountering certain laws that we may dislike or find offensive does not negate the existence of God or render the Bible outdated. Let me illustrate this with a couple of examples. The Bible teaches that God is a loving God, which resonates well with Americans because they like having a God who will forgive them of their failures. However, in the Middle East, this concept may be problematic. Conversely, consider the principle of no sex before marriage. While the Middle East may have no issue with it, Americans often take offense and consider it outdated.

When faced with a moral law that challenges us, it is essential to ask ourselves a fundamental question: if every person on the planet obeyed this law, would society be better off or worse off? Let us not question whether it will be difficult or whether all people can adhere to it. Instead, let us simply ponder whether society will be improved if we all follow it with a loving heart.

Furthermore, let us avoid introducing circumstances that make us argue against the moral law in question. For example, if the Bible teaches that marriage is intended for life, let us not immediately consider cases of spousal abuse and question whether it will be better for the victim to remain in that marriage. We must remember that the husband, in such a scenario, is not following God's law, thereby invalidating the example. In contemplating God's moral law, it is important to approach it with a broader perspective, seeking understanding and wisdom rather than dismissing it based on personal preferences or cultural differences.

In the 1950s, television shows would not dare depict even a married couple sharing the same bed. However, by the time I was a teenager, that had changed. Not only were married couples shown in the same bed but even unmarried couples were also portrayed sleeping together. In fact, there are countless shows today that label people who are not sexually active as having some sort of problem. It is a stark contrast to how things have been portrayed just a few decades ago. In today's TV shows, it often feels like the focus is on having as much sex as possible before getting married. And if the marriage does not work out, the solution seems to be getting a divorce and finding someone else.

I once had a friend ask me, "What if you wait until marriage and then find out the sex isn't satisfying?" I responded by saying that if both partners in the relationship waited until their wedding night, neither of them would have anything to compare it with. And looking back at my own first time, I was incredibly nervous, and when it was over, I thought it was good because I had nothing else to compare it with. It was like the first time I had ice cream. Even though it was just vanilla, I thought it was the best dessert I had ever tasted.

The same principle applies to a couple who waits until their wedding night to have sex. Neither of them will have prior experiences to compare it with, but the outcome will be incredible for both. What is even more amazing is that it will only get better as their marriage progresses. They will only have their own sexual relationship as a benchmark, and their wedding night will be a truly special, unforgettable experience that they will cherish for the rest of their lives.

O   O   O

In today's society, we often use new words and phrases to justify our actions, especially when it comes to sex. It allows us to feel better about ourselves and avoid guilt. Let me provide a few examples. In the past, if a man and woman had sex before marriage, it was referred to as sex out of wedlock or premarital sex. Nowadays we label it as *two consenting adults*. This new terminology not only sounds more acceptable but also implies that it is OK because both parties have agreed to it. However, in God's eyes, it simply means that two adults have agreed to engage in sin together. As the old saying goes, "Two wrongs do not make a right." We deceive ourselves by thinking that using creative words makes it OK and acceptable.

Similarly, in the past, if someone cheated on their spouse, it was called adultery, and there was shame associated with it. Today we use the term *affair*, which sounds much milder, eliminating the sense of shame. The person who has committed the offense may dismiss it by saying, "It didn't mean anything; it was just a little affair." Some even try to shift the blame onto their spouse. This is the kind of society we live in today.

I've once heard a pastor say that our culture has reached a point where no matter how horrific someone's actions are, they can always find a professor or expert from somewhere to justify it. Just look at abortion. Every day in our country, there are over two thousand abortions. Yet we have given it a new name: pro-choice or, ironically, planned parenthood. By adding positive words like *pro* or *planned* before *choice* or *parenthood*, we create a sense of righteousness around it. Sadly, we have lost the value of life in our country, resulting in thousands of abortions each day.

Not only do people actively support and advocate for these new terms but they even gather in large numbers, marching in the streets to defend and uphold them. It is intriguing to observe how passionately people rally behind these ideas. In reflecting on this phenomenon, it brings to mind the metaphor that Jesus has used to describe all of us as sheep. However, it is important to note that being likened to sheep is not intended as a compliment.

Sheep are widely known for their lack of intelligence, often considered one of the most unintelligent animals. Allow me to share an article I have come across years ago that exemplifies the foolishness of these creatures:

> In Istanbul, Turkey, a striking incident occurred where several hundred sheep mindlessly followed their leader off a cliff, resulting in a tragic plunge to their deaths. The incident took place in Van province, near Iran, as the shepherds from Ikizler village were engrossed in their breakfast, neglecting their responsibilities. This unfortunate lapse allowed the sheep to roam freely, ultimately leading to around 400 of them falling 15 meters into a ravine. Miraculously, their fall broke the descent for another 1,100 sheep, sparing their lives. Local newspaper reports estimated that the loss suffered by the farmers amounted to approximately $74,000.

This incident serves as a vivid illustration of the inherent foolishness and lack of discernment exhibited by sheep. Similarly, when we consider the collective actions of humans, it becomes evident that without proper guidance and discernment, we, too, can be easily swayed and led astray.

○ ○ ○

Pastor Matt of a Colorado Springs church I've attended has shared an insightful phrase with us that has stuck with me: "Fight for your heart so that you can fight with your heart." This statement holds a profound message. It emphasizes the importance of actively seeking and defending truth, enabling us to engage in battles armed with genuine understanding. It serves as a reminder that popularity and personal feelings do not necessarily equate to truth. If we are not vigilant, we risk falling into the same pattern as the sheep in the story, easily swayed and lacking discernment.

The pastor's words encourage us to cultivate a deep-rooted commitment to pursuing biblical truth. By diligently seeking and embracing what is genuinely true, we equip ourselves to engage with others, defend our convictions, and make informed decisions. It requires us to go beyond superficial appearances and popular opinions, to question, investigate, and wrestle with ideas to uncover the essence of biblical truth.

In a world filled with various ideologies and perspectives, fighting for our hearts means standing firm in our pursuit of truth, allowing it to shape our beliefs and guide our actions. Only then can we engage in meaningful conversations, challenge falsehoods, and ultimately contribute to a more enlightened and compassionate society.

O   O   O

The ongoing debate regarding abortion revolves around the question of when life begins. Does it begin at conception or at birth? I believe I can provide the correct answer to this question using scripture that you have probably never heard anyone use, but before I do, allow me to share a story.

When I was around twelve years old, I had a desire to earn some extra money to buy a pool table for our basement after watching a 1961 movie with my mother called *The Hustler*; it was about a pool shark. I came across an advertisement in a comic book that offered a way to make money by selling garden seeds. They would send me twenty small boxes containing various seeds like tomatoes, lettuce, corn, and more.

The plan was simple: after buying and reselling all the seeds, I would be left with a profit of $60. It seemed like a no-brainer.

Excited about the opportunity, I approached my father and asked him for a small loan to purchase the seeds. I promised to pay him back as soon as I made my first ten dollars. I managed to sell most of the boxes, and when I went back to my father to repay him, he surprised me. He expressed how proud he was of my entrepreneurial spirit and told me I only needed to pay him back five dollars. I was thrilled with his generosity.

Even after selling most of the boxes, I still had a couple left; that was when I approached my mother with another idea—I wanted to plant a garden in our backyard. To my delight, she not only agreed but also offered to help me. I think she, too, was proud of my initiative. So one Saturday afternoon, my mother and I ventured into the backyard to start our garden. We dedicated the entire day to working on it.

When my father saw what we were doing, he wanted to be a part of it as well. One evening he built a garden box and filled it with soil. He explained that we would plant the corn seeds in the box, and once they grew a couple of feet tall, we would transplant them into the garden in the backyard. He taught me how to plant the seeds using a thick stick to make a hole about three inches deep in the soil. Carefully, he dropped a single seed into each hole and covered it with soil.

My father emphasized the importance of watering the soil every morning as the plants needed water to grow. So every morning when I woke up, I would fetch a glass of water from the sink and gently pour it over the soil in the box.

The experience of starting my own garden and witnessing the growth of the plants became a cherished memory. It taught me the value of hard work and persistence and the joy of seeing something flourish from my hard work.

o   o   o

After just a few days, impatience started to creep in, and discouragement began to weigh heavily on me. Each day I would approach my father with the same question. "Are you sure everything is OK? I don't see any plants yet." And every time, he would respond with a gentle smile, asking if I had been faithfully watering the garden every morning. I assured him that I had been following his instructions diligently. He would then reassure me, saying, "Yes, I'm sure everything is OK. You just have to be patient."

Around a week into this waiting game, my father could sense my growing discouragement and the seeds of doubt taking root in my mind. Sensing the need to intervene, he walked over to the box we had placed in the kitchen floor. Kneeling, he beckoned me to come closer, saying, "Danny, I want to show you something." With careful hands, he began to remove the soil from a small area of the box. After clearing about an inch of soil, I caught a glimpse of a green tip emerging upward—a sign of life. He continued to excavate around it until he reached the bottom of the plant. Gently, he pulled it out, revealing what remained of the seed, torn apart, and transformed.

Looking at the plant in my father's hands, he posed a question to me, asking, "What does this look like?"

I replied, "A plant."

With a nod, he confirmed my answer and continued, "Yes, it's a plant. But you have to be patient and give it time to grow from the ground." Then he proceeded to explain the reason for placing the seed deep in the soil—to ensure that the roots would grow strong, providing a solid foundation for the towering plant to come.

His demonstration served as a profound lesson. It reminded me that new life takes time, that the process of transformation is often hidden beneath the surface. Just because I could not see the plant did not mean that there was no plant, so immediate results did not mean that progress was not happening. It was a reminder to trust in the unseen, to have faith in the potential within those tiny seeds.

From that moment on, I realized that nurturing my garden required patience, understanding that the journey of growth required time, care, and unwavering belief. And sure enough, with each passing day, the plants began to emerge from the soil, reaching toward the sun. It was a tangible manifestation of the beauty that can arise when we patiently cultivate what we have sown.

○   ○   ○

With that in mind, allow me to share a story in the Bible that serves as an illustration of when life begins. In John 12:24 (NIV), Jesus said, "Very truly I tell you the truth, unless a kernel of wheat falls to the ground and dies, it remains only a single seed. But if it dies, it produces many seeds."

While Jesus has used the example of a kernel of wheat to highlight our need to die to ourselves and find new life in him, it also offers insight into the beginning of life. His message conveys that if a seed is never planted, it remains as a seed indefinitely. However, when it is planted, it dies to itself and undergoes a transformative process; it becomes a plant even though you cannot see it, giving birth to numerous new seeds. The life of that plant commences the moment the seed dies or, in other words, breaks.

Reflecting on my father's act of planting corn seeds, I realized that had he not planted them, they would have perpetually remained as corn seeds. Yet by placing them in the soil and providing them with water, they died to their previous state and emerged as plants. Life for those corn plants began when the seeds shed their former selves and began to grow. As my father pulled one of the plants from the ground, revealing the split seed, it became evident that it was no longer just a seed. By sacrificing its original form, it had given rise to new life.

So when does life begin? It commences when a male sperm unites with a female egg, both sacrificing their individual identities. Once the sperm enters the womb and connects with the egg, they both relinquish their previous states. The sperm ceases to exist solely as a sperm, and the egg no longer remains merely an egg. Instead, they merge and form a union, dying to their former selves and initiating the beginning of life. Without this connection, the sperm and egg will persist as separate entities, never transforming into something more. Yet when they unite, they relinquish their previous identities to become life itself. And just because we cannot see the form of a baby yet does not mean there is no life.

This principle aligns precisely with God's intent for marriage, as articulated in Genesis 2:24 (NIV):

"For this reason, a man shall leave his father and his mother, and be joined to his wife, and they shall become one flesh."

The unity described here necessitates both partners being willing to undergo a metaphorical death to their former selves, including their single life and selfish tendencies. It involves a profound coming together to form a union where priorities shift from individual concerns to a collective focus on each other. In essence, the concept signifies that your spouse's joys and sorrows become your own, reflecting a shared life where any impact on your spouse deeply affects you. Failure to experience this symbiotic connection suggests that the transformative process of dying to oneself has not been fully realized.

○ ○ ○

When we employ the term *pro-choice* or *planned parenthood*, it becomes a mere euphemism, allowing us to engage in sexual activities without concern for potential consequences. It is a word that brings comfort, permitting us to make decisions about aborting a baby while evading responsibility. It is a word that eases our conscience and enables us to sleep at night. However, regardless of the words we use to justify our choices, abortion remains abortion—an act of terminating a life that has just begun and is in the process of being intricately formed by God's design.

> From birth I was cast upon you; from my mother's womb you have been my God. (Psalm 22:10, NIV)

> For you created my inmost being; you knit me together in my mother's womb. (Psalm 139:13, NIV)

○ ○ ○

It is intriguing to consider why many people desire to have their weddings take place in a church. I believe that the reason behind this inclination aligns with my own desire when I've gotten married—I want God's blessing. But do we genuinely believe that we can live life according to our own terms, be in a relationship, and then simply call on God to bless it on our wedding day? It seems that we have reduced God to a mere good-luck charm, only reaching out to him when we need something from him. He has become our personal secretary. It is rather audacious to think that the Creator of the universe, the God who has spoken everything into existence, will allow himself to be utilized as a tool for our personal gain.

Blaise Pascal once remarked that God created man in his image, and in return, man created God in his own image. As a society, we have not only molded God into our own likeness but also insulted him by convincing ourselves that we know better than God when it comes to determining what is morally right and wrong. We have concocted new words and phrases to give ourselves a sense of well-being, but in reality, we have strayed from God's ways, all the while assuming that we are still in good standing with him. Somehow, we have convinced ourselves that if enough people adopt our morals and values, God will simply align himself with our desires.

o   o   o

Now I could vividly recall the first time I met my first wife's family while we were still dating. We all gathered at a Houston restaurant, and immediately, I noticed that they were quite different from my own family. When I met her father, Bill, his imposing stature and firm handshake intimidated me. He resembled a figure reminiscent of John Wayne, and later I learned that he was an avid fan of the legendary actor. Bill was a godly man, and he embodied those old-fashioned values—a man of integrity whose word and handshake were as binding as a written contract. I truly admired him, and he would always insist on paying the bill whenever we went out to eat.

Terri's mother, Coco, stood in stark contrast to her husband's stature, much like Ronald and Nancy Reagan. Unfortunately, Bill passed away many years ago, and Coco is now living with one of her daughters. After our meal, as we made our way to the front door, Terri paused to embrace her parents tightly, expressing their love for one another. To my surprise, Terri extended the same affectionate gesture to her two sisters—they all hugged and exchanged the words *I love you*. I was taken aback yet deeply impressed. Such an act was foreign to my own family dynamics. In fact, the only time I hugged my parents after reaching my teenage years was upon my return from a yearlong stint in Korea, and even then, I did not embrace my siblings. It simply was not something we did.

The first time my father and I exchanged the words *I love you* was about a month before he passed away, and the only reason we did so was that we both knew he was nearing the end of his life. After becoming a father myself, I made a promise to tell my children every day that I love them. Even though my son is now in his thirties, I make it a point to express those three words every time we speak.

○   ○   ○

After a couple of months of being married, my now ex-wife and I visited her parents' house for dinner one evening as we often did. Her parents were always incredibly welcoming, making me feel like a part of their family from the very beginning. Despite being divorced from my ex-wife, I still maintain a wonderful relationship with Coco and Bill up until he passed away. For many years after the divorce, whenever they would introduce me to others, it would always be as their son-in-law. I also have a great rapport with my ex-wife, her current husband, and their daughter. It is a testament to the bond we have built over the years.

After dinner that night, my mother-in-law, Coco, brewed some coffee and suggested that we all retire to the living room—a customary post dinner routine at their house. It was already close to nine o'clock, and Coco proposed watching a movie. Although I knew I had to wake up early for work the next morning, I agreed, fully aware that I would not make it through the entire film. Coco produced a VHS tape and asked me, "Daniel, have you ever seen the movie *The Sound of Music?*" I replied I had not and asked what kind of movie it was. She proceeded to explain that it was based on a true story, transformed into a musical.

Now I had always considered myself a tough guy. I had served in the military as a military police officer, been part of a SWAT team in Korea—our unit was the first group of American soldiers to undergo ranger training in the Korean military—and even dabbled in bodybuilding after my military service. So naturally, the prospect of watching a musical that evening did not entice me. I glanced at Terri and silently mouthed my reluctance, careful not to let my in-laws overhear. I said, "I have to get up early for work."

Terri understood my sentiment perfectly and responded with a subtle lip gesture, signaling, "Let's just watch a little bit, OK?" Given my genuine fondness for my in-laws' company and a desire to be considerate, I acquiesced.

My mother-in-law excused herself and went into the kitchen, beckoning us to join her for a slice of pie she had prepared earlier that day. She suggested that we bring the pie into the living room and enjoy it while watching the movie. Cutting myself a rather generous piece (which, in my mind, was a fair reward for enduring this potentially agonizing film), I returned to the living room and took a seat next to my wife. My mother-in-law was quite the skilled cook, and this delectable pie was just what I needed to keep me engaged for the next thirty minutes or so.

As time passed and it neared ten o'clock, my wife leaned over and whispered in my ear, "Are you getting tired? Do we need to go?"

I turned to her and replied, "No, I'm OK. We can stay a little longer."

I thought, *This movie isn't as terrible as I anticipated.* I was also surprised to see Terri's father, who appeared to be a tough, old-fashioned-cowboy type, genuinely enjoying the movie.

Another thirty minutes went by, and my wife leaned over to me once again, whispering in my ear, "I know you're probably tired. If you want to go, we can leave."

I responded, "No, really. For some reason, I am not that tired yet. We can stay a little longer." The truth was I was feeling a bit fatigued that night, but I was genuinely starting to enjoy the movie and was eager to see how it would conclude. There was no way I was going to admit that to anyone.

Just a few minutes later, right in the middle of what seemed to be an intriguing part of the film, the VCR stopped, and my mother-in-law rose to remove the tape. I could not help but think, *How can the movie end in the middle of the story? That's the worst ending I've ever seen.*

So I asked, "Is it over?"

My mother-in-law replied, "Oh no, there's a second tape. It is a three-hour movie. But you do not have to stay. I know you have to wake up early for work in the morning."

As my wife sat beside me, believing that I was not enjoying the movie, she turned to her parents and said, "Maybe we should get going. Dan has to wake up early for work tomorrow."

Panic washed over me internally. I thought, *No, no, no, it is OK. We can't leave now.* There was absolutely no way I was going to walk out in the middle of this movie without knowing how it ended.

So I mustered up the courage and declared, "To be honest, I'm really not tired." I tried to downplay my enthusiasm for the movie, but I could not hide my desire to stay until the end.

With a deep voice, I looked at my mother-in-law and said, "Is there any more of that pie left?"

She kindly responded, "Sure, help yourself."

With a casual air, I strolled into the kitchen to fetch another slice of pie. As I did, I casually mentioned, "Go ahead and put in the second tape." I wanted to give the impression that my primary interest was indulging in another piece of pie rather than watching the movie.

Time passed, and the clock struck midnight. Finally, the movie concluded. I could not contain my excitement any longer and confessed to everyone how much I had truly enjoyed it. My mother-in-law could not believe that I had never seen the movie before, and she expressed her delight that I had found it enjoyable.

About a month later, my wife and I found ourselves once again at her parents' house for a dinner night. As we finished our meal, my in-laws suggested watching a movie, this time a John Wayne film. Normally, I had little interest in either musicals or those old-fashioned movies, finding it difficult to engage with them. However, to my surprise, the same thing happened with this movie as it had with *The Sound of Music*—I thoroughly enjoyed it and had no trouble staying up late, even knowing I had to work the next morning.

○   ○   ○

The reason I share these stories with you is to illustrate that love is very powerful. As I got to know my wife and her family better, something remarkable occurred. I began to undergo a transformation, slowly shedding my old self and embracing new preferences. I started to like the things they liked and dislike the things they disliked. I was becoming a different person.

This is precisely what happens when we develop a relationship with God. The more we come to know him, the more our tastes align with his, and our old self fades away, giving rise to a new life. Our perspectives shift, and we begin to see things through God's eyes.

There is a quote from C. S. Lewis that resonates deeply with me: "I believe in Christianity as I believe that the sun has risen, not only because I see it but because by it, I see everything else." The closer I grow to God, the more I see things the way he sees them, and with that comes profound changes in my life. Looking back, I can clearly see how I am no longer the same person. I no longer watch certain TV shows or listen to some of the music as before, and I definitely do not use the language I used to, and honestly, I am perfectly fine with that. I cherish the person that God is transforming me into, someone who prioritizes pleasing the One who has created me over self-gratification.

○   ○   ○

It is important for us to make sure we also have relationships with people who share the same beliefs as us as love holds significant power. When we spend time with someone who has opposing beliefs, the opposite effect can occur. The more we invest in that relationship, the greater the risk of being influenced and pulled away from our faith. Gradually, we might find ourselves developing a liking for things that are contrary to God's desires and that we have once held disdain for or, worse, ignorant of. This is exactly what happened to Solomon in the Old Testament, and because of it, his kingdom fell.

Jesus emphasized the connection between love and obedience in John 14:15–16 (NIV) when he said, "If you love me, keep my commands. And I will ask the Father, and he will give you another advocate to help you and be with you forever."

This profound statement reveals the essence of our relationship with him. Love acts as the driving force behind our desire to honor and obey him. When we genuinely love Jesus, it transforms our hearts and motivates us to live in accordance with his teachings. Our love for him becomes the compass that guides our thoughts, words, and actions.

In response to our love and obedience, Jesus assured us that the Father would send another advocate, the Holy Spirit, to be with us forever. This divine presence within us strengthens and empowers us to walk faithfully in his ways. The Holy Spirit, as our constant companion, provides guidance, comfort, and assistance in our journey of faith.

The intertwining of love, obedience, and the Holy Spirit's indwelling in our lives creates a powerful synergy. Love compels us to follow Christ's commands, and in turn, our obedience demonstrates the authenticity of our love. As we abide in his love and keep his commands, we experience the ongoing presence and support of the Holy Spirit, who enables us to live victoriously and fulfill God's purposes.

O   O   O

Being a tough guy is not merely about avoiding certain things or speaking in a certain manner. True toughness involves courage— the courage to stand for what is right, to believe in a Creator, and to live according to God's intended design for humanity rather than succumbing to the lure of justifying our actions with new words. Courage means calling things by their true names and standing firm in the face of adversity. Scripture not only encourages us to stand firm and be courageous in the pursuit of truth but commands us to do so. In the next chapter, I will delve further into the topic of courage.

It is crucial for us to grasp that God's desire for our lives is to let go of our old selves and embrace a new way of living, aligning ourselves with his will. He calls us to abandon our old lifestyles and adopt his way of life. His ultimate desire is for us to become like his Son and to be distinct from the rest of the world. This is why 2 Corinthians 3:18 (NIV) states:

> And we all, who with unveiled faces contemplate the Lord's glory, are being transformed into his image with ever-increasing glory, which comes from the Lord, who is the Spirit.

This is what Jesus was talking when Nicodemus privately asked him about the kingdom of heaven.

> He came to Jesus at night and said, "Rabbi, we know that you are a teacher who has come from God. For no one could perform the signs you are doing if God were not with him."
> Jesus replied, "Very truly I tell you, no one can see the kingdom of God unless they are born again."
> "How can someone be born when they are old?" Nicodemus asked. "Surely they cannot enter a second time into their mother's womb to be born!"
> Jesus answered, "Very truly I tell you, no one can enter the kingdom of God unless they are born of water and the Spirit. Flesh gives birth to flesh, but the Spirit gives birth to spirit. You should not be surprised at my saying, 'You must be born again.' The wind blows wherever it pleases. You hear its sound, but you cannot tell where it comes from or where it is going. So it is with everyone born of the Spirit." (John 3:2–8, NIV)

One of the greatest challenges within Christianity is that many people claim to be Christians, yet their lives show no discernible difference from those who do not profess faith in God. I find it hard to believe that when the Holy Spirit enters someone's life, there will be no transformation whatsoever. Such a lack of change indicates that the Holy Spirit has failed to bring about the desired transformation in that person, and that cannot be the case. That is why in the book James it says this.

What good is it, my brothers and sisters, if someone claims to have faith but has no deeds? Can such faith save them? Suppose a brother or sister is without clothes and daily food. If one of you says to them, "Go in peace; keep warm and well fed," but does nothing about their physical needs, what good is it? (James 2:14-16, NIV)

True Christianity involves a personal ongoing transformation where our lives increasingly reflect the character of Christ. As we yield ourselves to the leading of the Holy Spirit, he works within us, molding us into the likeness of Jesus. This transformation is a lifelong process, marked by the continuous growth of Christ's glory within us.

O   O   O

The narrative of Jesus raising Lazarus from the dead beautifully parallels the concept of being born again. In John 11:43 as Jesus calls out loudly, *"Lazarus, come out!"* and Lazarus emerges from the tomb, we witness a profound transformation. Yet, the process does not end there; it is just the beginning.

Jesus then instructs those present to do something remarkable: *"Take off the grave clothes and let him go."* This moment holds a deep symbolic meaning. Similarly, when we experience spiritual rebirth, we embark on a journey of shedding our old, entangled ways – our "grave clothes." But the beauty lies in the fact that these instructions are not directed towards Lazarus, he was bound with strips of linen from head to toe. They are meant for the people around him – a subtle reminder that often, we are blinded by our old self, unable to see what needs to be removed from our lives.

So, how do we embark on this transformative journey? We are guided by insightful teachers, pastors, and fellow believers who illuminate the truth. They help us navigate the complexities of shedding our old habits and embracing our new identity in Christ. Just as the people around Lazarus aided in removing his grave clothes, our spiritual companions help us free ourselves from the trappings of our past, allowing us to fully embrace the new life that being born again offers.

It is important for us to examine our own lives and assess whether we are truly being transformed by the Holy Spirit. If we claim to follow Christ, there should be evident changes in our attitudes, actions, and values that not only do we notice but others notice them as well. These changes may only be baby steps, but our lives should increasingly align with God's Word and reflect his love, grace, and righteousness. Let us continually seek his presence and surrender to his transformative work in our lives, allowing his Spirit to bring about lasting change.

○   ○   ○

I have often heard people say, "My Christianity is a personal matter." It is true that our relationship with God is indeed personal. This is why Jesus has said this in the book of Matthew:

> And when you pray, do not be like the hypocrites, for they love to pray standing in the synagogues and on the street corners to be seen by others. Truly I tell you, they have received their reward in full. But when you pray, go into your room, close the door, and pray to your Father, who is unseen. Then your Father, who sees what is done in secret, will reward you. (Matthew 6:5–6, NIV)

While our relationship with God is personal, we must understand that our Christianity is anything but personal. Our Christian faith is meant to be lived out publicly. In the book of Matthew, God calls us to be the salt of the earth and the light of the world:

You are the salt of the earth. But if the salt loses its saltiness, how can it be made salty again? It is no longer good for anything, except to be thrown out and trampled underfoot.

You are the light of the world. A city situated on a hill cannot be hidden. Nor do people light a lamp and put it under a basket, but on a lampstand, and it gives light to all who are in the house. Let your light so shine before others, that they may see your good deeds and glorify your Father in heaven. (Matthew 5:13–16, NIV)

Jesus teaches us that a city situated on a hill cannot be hidden. When we have a genuine relationship with Christ and are filled with the light of the Holy Spirit, it becomes evident to those around us. This visibility stems from the fact that our lives begin to diverge from the norms of the world. Our actions and choices become distinct, drawing the attention of others. God calls his people to live in a way that stands apart from the rest of the world.

As followers of Christ, we are called to be different—to exemplify his love, grace, and truth in our daily lives. Our faith should shine brightly, not hidden away. When we live in accordance with God's principles, our actions and deeds become a testament to his transformative power. Others will notice the difference, and some will be drawn to glorify our heavenly Father.

Therefore, let us embrace the call to live distinctively as followers of Christ, allowing his light to illuminate our lives and affect those around us. May our actions and deeds serve as a testimony to God's love and goodness, bringing glory to him in all that we do.

As we strive to live a life aligned with God's standards rather than our own, we will find that sometimes God allows our faith to be tested. Let me share an example that illustrates this.

Years ago, I made the decision to sell my SUV through an online platform. Coincidentally, during that same week while driving down a road, I encountered a huge pothole. Immediately, I sensed that something was off. While others might not have noticed any issue during a test-drive, I, having driven the truck for three years, knew that something was not right. Despite my attempts to dismiss it, I could not escape the voice of God's Word echoing in my mind. It felt like a challenge, testing whether everything I knew and taught would be applied in my own life, even when it meant bearing unexpected expenses.

You see, I had faced significant hardships and accumulated substantial debt over the past few years. Therefore, my primary goal was to sell and eliminate the payment and use what was left over to pay off some debt. However, deep down, I recognized there was only one right course of action.

The following day, I scheduled an appointment with an automotive shop to have my SUV examined. I did not want to make a big deal out of it, but that afternoon, I asked my brother (who worked with me in the same office) if he could meet me at the automotive shop after work. I needed a ride back home, and he gladly agreed.

Since my brother would leave the office about thirty minutes earlier than I would, I informed one of the other managers that I needed to leave work a bit early that day. Concerned, he asked if everything was all right. I assured him that it was, explaining that I had to take my car to the automotive shop and that my brother would meet me there to provide a ride home. Curiously, he remarked, "I thought you were selling the vehicle." I confirmed his assumption and narrated the incident with the pothole, expressing my conviction that doing the right thing meant getting it checked and repaired, if necessary, before selling it.

This conversation took place within earshot of other coworkers, who could not resist sharing their thoughts. One suggested, "Dan, why not just lower the price by a couple of hundred bucks?"

I responded, "But what if the repair costs exceed a couple of hundred dollars?"

Another chimed in, "Well, that's the new owner's problem."

Then someone else proposed, "Dan, if it runs and the issue isn't noticeable, just sell it and let the new owner deal with it. That's what everyone else does."

Firmly, I replied, "I don't want to be like everybody else. I would not want someone to do that to me."

At this point, a coworker sitting in the adjacent cubicle, who had been quietly listening, stood up with a smile and said, "Hey, Dan, let me know next time you decide to sell something. Maybe my wife and I would be interested in buying it."

Reflecting on the conversation at work and the coworker's remark about being interested in buying something from me in the future, I cannot help but ponder the significance of doing what is right in the eyes of God. Should not that be our natural inclination as followers of Christ? Yet too often, we prioritize our own interests and make excuses, justifying our behavior by claiming it is what everyone else does. But God's call for us is not to be like everyone else; rather, he beckons us to stand out, to be different.

> Do not conform to the pattern of this world, but be transformed by the renewing of your mind. Then you will be able to test and approve what God's will is—his good, pleasing and perfect will. (Romans 12:2, NIV)

o   o   o

The following day, when I received the call from the automotive shop about the repair costs, my heart sank. They informed me that fixing my SUV would amount to almost eleven hundred dollars. I felt a knot in my stomach. In a moment of uncertainty, I asked, "What if I choose not to fix it?"

The shop attendant responded, "Well, you can still drive it, but eventually, it will break down on you." I wrestled with the decision, unsure of what to do. Yet deep within my heart, a question persisted: what is the right thing to do? Sometimes doing what is right comes at a cost. It may require sacrificing our money, our time, our popularity, or even our life in some parts of the world.

So in times of adversity, when you find yourself facing difficult challenges and weighing your options, remember the powerful words of James.

Consider it pure joy, my brothers and sisters, whenever you face trials of many kinds, because you know that the testing of your faith produces perseverance. Let perseverance finish its work so that you may be mature and complete, not lacking anything. (James 1:2–4

Embrace these verses and recognize that choosing to do what is right, even when it demands sacrifice, holds tremendous rewards in your journey with Christ.

In the book of James, he encourages us to consider it a source of pure joy when we encounter trials of various kinds. Why? Because these trials serve as tests for our faith, refining and strengthening us through perseverance. As we endure and allow perseverance to complete its work within us, we are transformed, maturing and becoming whole, lacking nothing.

It is important to grasp the deeper meaning behind these verses. They remind us that our faith is not exempt from challenges or hardships. Rather, these obstacles serve as opportunities for growth, deepening our character and shaping us into the people God intends us to be. By embracing trials with joy and maintaining our commitment to righteousness, we align ourselves with God's plan for our lives.

So the next time you find yourself in the midst of a difficult situation, remember the wisdom of James. Embrace the trials, knowing that they have the potential to refine your faith, cultivate perseverance, and lead you to a place of maturity and completeness in Christ. Trust in God's guidance and allow his transformative work to unfold in your life.

o　o　o

It is crucial to recognize that doing what is right becomes easier when there is an audience, but true integrity is displayed when no one is watching. We must learn to stand firm in our commitment to righteousness even in the absence of external scrutiny. For instance, when it comes to filing taxes, it is important to uphold complete honesty. While utilizing tax laws to one's advantage is legitimate, distorting the truth to maximize returns is a different matter entirely.

Throughout my life, I have encountered people who run side businesses and have heard some justify questionable practices, such as claiming family vacations as business expenses. When I've raised concerns, they will argue that since they have briefly discussed business matters during the trip, it's qualified as a business expense. Common sense tells us that something is amiss in such justifications. We need to develop the fortitude to do what is right and truthful, even when no one is watching because even when we believe we are unseen, the One who truly matters is observing.

I would rather experience failure while standing firm in righteousness, knowing that I am aligned with God's will, than fail while engaging in dishonesty or manipulation. When we fail while pursuing what is right, we can find peace, understanding that it may not have been God's plan for our lives. However, when we fail due to deceitful actions, we must face the consequences and question whether God is disciplining us for our lack of integrity.

As John Wooden wisely stated, "Be more concerned with your character than your reputation, for your character is who you truly are, while your reputation is merely others' perception of you." Remember: our true character shines brightest when no one is watching. It is in those unseen moments that our integrity and commitment to doing what is right truly define us.

o   o   o

Another challenging attribute that God calls us to apply in our lives is forgiveness. What does it mean to truly forgive someone according to God? Let me illustrate this with an example I've learned from

Pastor Matt. At some point in our lives, each of us has experienced a disagreement or conflict in a relationship. Whether it is with a friend, coworker, or romantic partner, there are times when words or actions cause offense or hurt. In many instances, these disagreements are minor and can be resolved through communication. However, there are instances when someone's words or actions deeply offend or wound us, creating a divide between us and the other person.

In such situations, our character determines how we respond. Some people may lay out the welcome mat to extend a tentative welcome, requiring the other person to initiate reconciliation. Others may build a white picket fence, allowing themselves to be in the same room as the other just as long as boundaries are maintained. Some erect tall walls, ensuring they never have to see or interact with the other person, going to great lengths to avoid any encounter. Some people will put it in their holster, and they pull it out later when they need something or trying to prove a point. Then there are those who construct a metaphorical boxing ring, seeking revenge to the other person.

However, God calls us to follow the example of his Son. Jesus has come to build bridges and to forgive. This lesson of forgiveness is of utmost importance, one that we must truly grasp. Why is it so crucial? That is an excellent question to ponder. Have you ever prayed the Lord's Prayer? Perhaps you have recited it or heard it being recited, but have you ever truly listened to its words?

In Matthew 6:9–13 (NIV), Jesus teaches us how to pray, and within this prayer, he emphasizes forgiveness:

> Our Father in heaven,
> Hallowed be Your name.
> Your kingdom come,
> Your will be done,
> On earth as it is in heaven.
> Give us this day our daily bread.
> And forgive us our debts,
> *As we also have forgiven our debtors.* (Emphasis added)

I consider verse 6 in the Lord's prayer to be the second most alarming passages in the Bible, compelling even believers to pause and examine themselves. Within this powerful prayer, we are actually saying to God to forgive us of our debts as we forgive others. That is an eye-opening statement. It is a reminder that our relationship with God is intricately connected to our relationships with others. To truly experience God's forgiveness and walk in his righteousness, we must be willing to extend forgiveness to those who have hurt us, no matter how bad.

Forgiveness is not merely a casual act; it is a transformative process that frees us from the bondage of bitterness and allows us to experience healing and restoration. As we forgive, we align ourselves with God's heart and reflect his love and mercy to the world. It is a vital lesson that we must learn and apply in our lives, for through forgiveness, we embrace the path of true reconciliation and peace.

Now some of you may have reservations or questions regarding the Lord's Prayer and the concept of forgiveness. You may be thinking, *that's not exactly what we're saying in that prayer.* It is important to explore this further and examine what Jesus says immediately after teaching us the prayer.

In Matthew 6:14–15 (NIV), Jesus clarifies the significance of forgiveness:

> For if you forgive other people when they sin against you, your heavenly Father will also forgive you. But if you do not forgive others their sins, your Father will not forgive your sins.

These words spoken by Jesus carry tremendous weight and invite us to reflect on the gravity of forgiveness. It is a call to take forgiveness seriously and to learn how to forgive in the same manner as God forgives us.

God's forgiveness is profound and unconditional, offered to us freely through his grace. However, Jesus highlights the connection between our forgiveness of others and receiving forgiveness from our heavenly Father. It is not a matter of earning or deserving forgiveness but rather a transformative aspect of our relationship with God.

By extending forgiveness to those who have wronged us, we align ourselves with God's heart and emulate his love and mercy. In doing so, we open ourselves to experiencing the depth of God's forgiveness and the healing and freedom it brings. On the other hand, if we withhold forgiveness and harbor resentment, we hinder the flow of God's forgiveness in our lives.

o　　o　　o

For those of you who are thinking, *I cannot forgive this person. You have no idea what he or she has done to me*, let me share a little-known story about Adolph Coors IV, a member of the Coors beer family in Colorado, that sheds light on the power of forgiveness.

In 1960, when Adolph was just fourteen years old, his father was tragically kidnapped and brutally murdered. It was an unimaginable pain and loss that he had to bear. Years later, in 1975, Adolph had a profound encounter with Christ that transformed his life. And in 1977, something remarkable happened. He met face-to-face with Joseph Corbett, the man responsible for his father's abduction and murder. Instead of harboring bitterness and seeking revenge, Adolph chose to forgive him.

In reflecting on his journey of forgiveness, Adolph Coors said this:

> Did you ever stop to think that the person who hurt you so deeply may have been God's agent in your life, sent there by God to bring you into a growing experience, so you could learn how to walk in forgiveness.
>
> No, God is not the author of evil, but God seeing the bad thing in this person's character, and seeing someone who was not growing, seeing you as someone who did not know the first thing about forgiveness, decided, I am going to bring these two people together.

This story serves as a powerful reminder that forgiveness has the potential to transcend the darkest moments of our lives. It is a choice that allows us to release the burden of anger and resentment and, in doing so, experience true freedom and healing. Adolph Coors's journey teaches us that forgiveness is not a sign of weakness but rather a courageous act that opens the door to growth, restoration, and ultimately a deep sense of peace in our Christian journey.

○　○　○

Indeed, an essential aspect of true forgiveness is the act of erasing what's happened to live in a manner as if the offense never occurred at all. The concept of this kind of forgiveness is beautifully expressed in Psalm 103:11–12 (NIV):

> For as the heavens are high above the earth,
> So great is His mercy toward those who fear Him;
> As far as the east is from the west,
> So far has He removed our transgressions from us.

In these verses, we witness the magnitude of God's forgiveness and the depth of his compassion. God's nature is characterized by his boundless compassion, grace, and love. Unlike human beings who often hold grudges and seek revenge, God does not treat us as our sins deserve or repay us according to our iniquities.

The psalmist further illustrates the extent of God's forgiveness by using a powerful metaphor: "As far as the east is from the west, so far has he removed our transgressions from us." This imagery conveys the immeasurable distance between our sins and God's forgiveness. When God forgives us, he completely removes our transgressions from us, separating them infinitely from his presence.

To truly understand and practice forgiveness, we are called to emulate the divine model presented in Psalm 103. Just as God forgives us and removes our sins from us, we are encouraged to extend the same grace and mercy to others. True forgiveness involves letting go of resentment, releasing the desire for retribution, and embracing a mindset that allows for complete reconciliation.

While it may be challenging to erase the memory of the offense, forgiveness entails cultivating a heart that no longer holds the offense against the wrongdoer. It means choosing to treat the other person with kindness, compassion, and love as if the offense had never occurred. This does not diminish the pain or consequences of the offense, but it acknowledges our willingness to move forward without harboring bitterness or seeking vengeance.

As followers of Christ, we are called to reflect his character by embodying forgiveness. By doing so, we participate in the divine work of healing, restoration, and reconciliation. May we be inspired by the words of Psalm 103 and strive to practice forgiveness in its fullest sense, imitating the boundless grace and love of our heavenly Father.

○   ○   ○

As a father, I have experienced firsthand the power of love and forgiveness in a parent-child relationship. When my son was a young boy, I had to discipline him for his actions. Immediately after the discipline, I made it a point to embrace him tightly, expressing my love for him and assuring him of my forgiveness. I made a conscious effort not to bring up his wrongdoing again, letting the incident fade into the past.

There is one particular moment that remains etched in my memory, although I cannot recall the exact details of what has caused my disappointment. However, I was determined not to let my feelings of frustration overshadow my love for my son. So after I disciplined him, a few moments passed, and to my surprise, he looked up at me and asked, "Aren't you going to hug me and tell me you forgive me?"

My heart melted at his innocent request, and without hesitation, I responded, "Of course," holding him even tighter in a prolonged embrace.

I gently pulled him away from me, gazing into his eyes, and sincerely said, "Yes, I forgive you." In that moment, my son knew the genuineness of my forgiveness and felt the warmth of my love.

This simple yet profound exchange taught me an invaluable lesson about the power of forgiveness and its impact on a child's heart. By extending forgiveness and expressing unconditional love, I created an environment of safety and security for my son. He understood that even in the midst of discipline, my love for him remained unwavering. Through this experience, I learned that forgiveness is not merely a transactional act but also a transformative one. It has the ability to mend wounds, restore relationships, and foster a sense of trust and emotional well-being.

In our journey of faith, we can draw parallels from this father-child dynamic. Just as I have exemplified forgiveness as a father, God, our heavenly Father, extends his forgiveness to us with boundless love. When we sincerely seek his forgiveness for our transgressions, he embraces us with open arms, assuring us of his unconditional love. He does not hold our past mistakes against us but forgives us completely, allowing us to experience the freedom and renewal that forgiveness brings.

The profound truth is that God's forgiveness is even greater than a human father's love. His love knows no bounds, and his forgiveness erases our sins completely, offering us a fresh start. When we approach God with a repentant heart, desiring his forgiveness, we can trust that his response is one of unwavering love and genuine forgiveness.

I want to emphasize that I do not claim to be a perfect father; in fact, I am far from it. I have made my fair share of mistakes along the way, and I continue to do so. However, by implementing this essential lesson in our relationship, my son always knows the sincerity of my forgiveness and understands the depth of my unconditional love for him. It is my hope that each of us can truly comprehend the profound nature of God's forgiveness in our own lives.

As we approach God with humility, seeking his forgiveness, we can rest assured that his response goes far beyond mere acceptance. He not only embraces us but also runs to us with open arms, just as illustrated in Jesus's parable of the prodigal son. God's love and grace know no bounds, and his forgiveness is immeasurable.

There is another understanding of forgiveness that we need to comprehend. Throughout my Christian journey, there had been numerous occasions in my life when I dined out with friends, family, or even church members where we experienced poor service in several instances. It often happened after attending Sunday morning service during the rush. The waiter or waitress would apologize, explaining that they were understaffed. Despite their apology, some of us would still feel upset. Some members of the group would leave a meager tip to show their displeasure even after the waiter or waitress apologized, and some would expect some form of compensation, such as a discount or a free dessert. I used to think the same way, but I have come to understand the true essence of forgiveness.

Genuine forgiveness entails accepting the apology and then completely erasing the offense as if it has never happened. How can I possibly expect something in return if I have truly forgiven the person? Demanding compensation or seeking personal gain in exchange for forgiveness only reveals that I have never truly forgiven them. It is merely a transaction, not an act of genuine forgiveness.

It is in moments like these that God presents us with tremendous opportunities to reflect his Son and make a lasting impact on those who have offended us. Just imagine the next time you encounter poor service, and the manager approaches you and sincerely apologizes, acknowledging that the service should never have been subpar, and then offers a gesture of appreciation by suggesting a 25 percent or more discount on your bill. But instead of eagerly accepting the discount, you respond with a gracious spirit, saying, "I genuinely appreciate your apology, and I accept it wholeheartedly. However, there is no need to take anything off my bill. You see, if Jesus can freely forgive me of all my sins, then I can extend that same forgiveness to you. So there is no need to give me a discount. Please just give me the full bill."

In this scenario, you exemplify the transformative power of forgiveness and demonstrate a Christlike attitude of love and grace to not only the manager but anyone else who happens to hear it as well. By refusing the discount, you convey a message that forgiveness is not contingent on receiving something in return. It is an act of compassion and mercy freely given, just as Christ has freely forgiven us. I have done this many times after learning this lesson, and to see the look on people's faces is priceless.

○   ○   ○

As I have mentioned before, Jesus has come to bridge the gap in our relationship with him, and he also desires us to learn how to build bridges in our relationships with others. This principle is beautifully illustrated in Luke, where Jesus teaches us to love our enemies, do good, and lend without expecting anything in return.

In Luke 6:35–36 (NIV), Jesus says, "But love your enemies, do good to them, and lend to them without expecting to get anything back. Then your reward will be great, and you will be children of the Most High, because he is kind to the ungrateful and wicked. Be merciful, just as your Father is merciful." This passage conveys two important lessons when we follow Jesus's example to lend without expecting anything in return.

1. It protects the one who is lending money, meaning we should never lend money that we cannot afford to lose, but rather, if we have the capacity to lend without expecting repayment, we should do so. It is about selflessly offering assistance and support to others without putting them under pressure to fulfill our expectations. And FYI, according to Exodus 22:25-27, we should never charge interest when lending money; this is a big no-no in God's eyes. We should not seek personal gain from others' misfortune.

2. When we lend with no expectation of repayment, something remarkable happens. There is no divide or strain in the relationship if the other person is not able to pay back what they have borrowed. The bridge between us remains intact, fostering a deeper connection and understanding. Moreover, the person who receives our generosity is grateful that we never bring up the debt, even if they may feel guilty for not being able to repay it at the time.

By following Jesus's teachings in this regard, we demonstrate a profound love and grace toward others. We embody the character of our heavenly Father, who shows kindness even to the ungrateful and the wicked. Our actions reflect a genuine desire to build bridges of reconciliation and understanding, just as Jesus has done for us.

So let us embrace this teaching and extend a helping hand, lend without expectation, and love others unconditionally. In doing so, we align ourselves with the heart of Christ and become agents of his transformative love in the world.

○   ○   ○

There are several issues plaguing churches today that need thoughtful consideration and address: The rise of prosperity-focused churches is a concerning trend. These churches often teach a message centered on personal success and tapping into one's inner self to achieve prosperity. However, this approach neglects the harsh reality faced by many faithful believers, including the persecution experienced by early disciples and countless Christians worldwide throughout history. Such churches shy away from discussing sin, our desperate need for a Savior, and the importance of aligning our thoughts with God's. They also tend to overlook Jesus's crucial message of being born again.

The issue with prosperity churches lies in their emphasis on motivational speeches rather than imparting the true teachings of the Gospel. This lack of authentic Gospel teaching can have profound and lasting consequences. While these pastors may excel at inspiring their congregations to pursue success and worldly achievements, they often neglect the crucial aspect of transforming lives to reflect Christ's teachings.

Leaving these churches, one may feel empowered with a mindset geared toward worldly success, even the aspiration to conquer the world. However, the crucial focus on personal transformation and becoming more Christlike is often missing. The absence of genuine Gospel teachings means that, despite the large number of attendees and the apparent success, it can merely be the blind leading the blind, lacking the spiritual foundation required to build a deep and meaningful relationship with God.

Moreover, prosperity churches often falter when it comes to upholding God's moral law. Instead of standing firmly on the truth of God's Word, they tend to compromise and adapt to societal trends, losing sight of biblical principles. This adaptability may make them popular and accepted by the world, but it compromises the integrity of their message and dilutes the true essence of Christianity.

In contrast, genuine Christian faith should inspire believers to embrace transformation and holiness, not merely success in worldly endeavors. True churches teach the complete Gospel, urging people to align their lives with God's will and to seek righteousness in all things. This foundation allows believers to stand firm, anchored in God's truth, and resist the allure of worldly temptations. Only through a comprehensive understanding and application of the Gospel can we find genuine spiritual growth and lasting fulfillment in our faith journey.

o   o   o

Conversely, there is another problem in some churches—an overemphasis on grace without addressing the responsibility of believers. While discussing God's amazing grace is crucial, focusing solely on it can lead to a false sense of security for those who attend church occasionally without genuine transformation. We must strike a balance between understanding God's amazing grace and recognizing our accountability to his teachings.

In 1 Corinthians 3:10–15 (NIV), Paul addresses the concept of accountability among Christians.

> By the grace God has given me, I laid a foundation as a wise builder, and someone else is building on it. But each one should build with care. For no one can lay any foundation other than the one already laid, which is Jesus Christ. If anyone builds on this foundation using gold, silver, costly stones, wood, hay or straw, their work will be shown for what it is, because the Day will

bring it to light. It will be revealed with fire, and the fire will test the quality of each person's work. If what has been built survives, the builder will receive a reward. If it is burned up, the builder will suffer loss but yet will be saved—even though only as one escaping through the flames.

Paul emphasizes that on the Day of Judgment, the quality of each person's work will be tested through fire. Those who have built their lives on a foundation of righteousness will be rewarded, while those whose actions are found wanting will suffer loss. It is essential to comprehend that this accountability is not related to salvation but rather to the actions and choices we make as followers of Christ.

I've recently heard a pastor respond to those who have questioned his emphasis on grace by affirming that it is not him but rather them who struggle with accepting God's grace. The reality is that true salvation involves a profound change in our lives, and without the teaching of our accountability, that may not happen. If one hears every week only about God's grace, then what is the motivation for someone to examine themselves to see if they are truly in the faith as Paul suggests in the second book of Corinthians?

In conclusion, churches must strike a balance in their teachings. While embracing God's grace is paramount, it should not overshadow the importance of genuine transformation, personal responsibility, and accountability for our actions as followers of Christ. By understanding this balance, churches can create an environment that nurtures true spiritual growth and discipleship among its members.

o   o   o

Being different as followers of Christ goes beyond outward symbols like wearing a Christian T-shirt, a fish symbol ring, or a cross necklace. True differentiation lies in living a life that reflects Christ. Jesus was profoundly different because he consistently acted contrary to societal norms. He engaged with people whom others would typically avoid, and he extended forgiveness even when it seemed undeserved. Even when Jesus was beaten and crucified, he did not seek revenge but instead prayed for his persecutors.

It is crucial to recognize that many people mistakenly believe they have a relationship with God simply because they recite prayers before meals or bedtime. While there is value in expressing gratitude and seeking God's guidance through these rituals, they alone do not deepen our relationship with him.

First Samuel 15:22 (NIV) tells us, "To obey is better than sacrifice." The more we spend time in scripture, the more we get to know him; and the more we get to know him, the more it affects how we approach these practices. It transforms the way we offer a blessing before a meal or engage in prayer as our knowledge of God shapes our hearts and intentions.

Authentic Christianity involves living in a way that mirrors Christ's character and teachings. It encompasses genuine connection and transformation, going beyond superficial acts of religious observance. By seeking to truly know God, we can experience a profound change that influences every aspect of our lives and the way we relate to others.

○   ○   ○

I once worked for a company in Atlanta, Georgia, where my boss, Victor, displayed an interesting contradiction. Victor was generally a pleasant person, but he had a tendency to use profanity akin to a drunken sailor. It always struck me as peculiar when we gathered for lunch in the company kitchen, and Victor would bow his head, close his eyes, and say a brief prayer before his meal. After this prayer, he would make the sign of the cross with his right hand in the Catholic tradition. However, within just a minute or two of resuming the conversation with whoever he was sitting with, he would inevitably revert to using offensive language. Witnessing this behavior, I could not help but wonder how someone who had just prayed to God could so casually use such vulgar language.

This experience serves as a reminder that our actions speak louder than our rituals or words. It highlights the importance of genuine transformation in our hearts and the consistency between our beliefs and behavior. While Victor's prayer and sign of the cross may have been a sincere expression of his faith in those moments, the stark contrast between his actions and his profanity-laden speech raises questions about the authenticity of his spiritual journey. It reminds me that our relationship with God should encompass more than external rituals; it should reflect a genuine transformation that influences how we speak, treat others, and conduct ourselves in everyday life.

About a year into my job, Victor contacted me, informing me that he would be coming to Houston to accompany me on client visits. Shortly after picking him up from the airport, he uttered some explicit words that I preferred not to repeat. As the day progressed and I dropped him off at his hotel, he looked at me and offered an apology for his earlier use of profanity. He acknowledged that I was a Christian and did not curse, but he claimed it was just the way he was. I responded, "Victor, you shouldn't worry about what I think since you are my boss. However, I believe you should be concerned about what God thinks because one day you will stand before him and be held accountable." This prompted him to embark on a speech about how God does not really care about the words people use, considering them merely man-made constructs from years ago.

I then presented him with a scenario. I mentioned his daughter, who was around eight years old at the time and occasionally visited the office with his wife. I asked if he would be OK with me speaking to his daughter the way he spoke with me since, according to his argument, they were just made-up words. He responded by saying it was different because she was just a little girl, and he did not want his daughter to adopt his way of speaking. Frustrated, he replied that there were words for adults and words for kids. I then pointed out that if the words were only distinguished by age, he would eventually be OK with me using such language with his daughter once she turned eighteen.

By this point, Victor was growing more exasperated and challenged me to show him in the Bible where God explicitly forbade the use of the particular word he used. I acknowledged that the word did not exist during biblical times, so I could not provide a direct reference regarding that specific word. However, I emphasized that God did not want him to speak like a drunken sailor. He proposed a deal, stating that if I could show him in the Bible that God disapproved of his manner of speech, he would cease using such language. I agreed to his proposition, saying, "OK, deal."

o   o   o

That night I went home determined to do my homework and be prepared for my discussion with Victor the next morning. I knew he had doubted that I would find anything to prove him wrong, but I was determined to present my case. As I picked up Victor from the hotel the following morning, I made sure to have my Bible sitting prominently on the passenger seat. When he opened the car door and saw the Bible, a grin appeared on his face. He picked it up and asked, "So did you find anything?"

With confidence, I responded, "I bookmarked a few pages and highlighted the verses I'd like you to read." As I handed him the Bible, I pulled out of the parking lot and began our twenty-minute drive to our first appointment. Victor opened the Bible to the marked pages and started reading the verses I had selected.

> Do not let any unwholesome talk come out of your mouths, but only what is helpful for building others up according to their needs, that it may benefit those who listen. (Ephesians 4:29, NIV)

> Make a tree good and its fruit will be good, or make a tree bad and its fruit will be bad, for a tree is recognized by its fruit. You brood of vipers, how can you who are evil say anything good? For out of the overflow of the heart the mouth speaks. The good man brings good things out of the good stored up in him, and the evil man brings evil things out of the evil stored up in him. But I tell you that men will have to give account on the day of judgment for every careless word they have spoken. For by your words you will be acquitted,

and by your words you will be condemned. (Matthew
12:33–37, NIV)

A good man brings good things out of the good stored
up in his heart, and an evil man brings evil things out
of the evil stored up in his heart. For the mouth speaks
what the heart is full of. (Luke 6:45, NIV)

As I drove the car, I could see Victor engrossed in reading the
verses from Ephesians first, and then he turned to the book of Matthew,
delving into the highlighted passages. It was as if he was in a trance,
completely absorbed in the words. After finishing Matthew, he turned
back to Ephesians, reading the verses before and after the ones I had
highlighted. Perhaps he was hoping to find something that would
discredit my chosen verses and prove them out of context. He followed
the same process with the Matthew verses.

For about fifteen minutes, there was silence, broken only by the
sound of his reading. Finally, he looked up at me and said, "I never
knew the Bible talked about stuff like this."

I responded by asking, "Have you ever taken the time to read it?"

He paused for a few seconds, contemplating the question, and
admitted, "To be honest, no."

I continued, "Isn't it interesting how people who want to go on a
diet will buy a book on how to lose weight and spend days or weeks
reading it cover to cover, applying everything they learn to achieve
their weight loss goals? Or how those who aspire to be successful will
purchase a book on how to make money, reading it diligently and
implementing the recommended strategies for success? Here we have a
book that tells us how to save our souls, how to attain eternal life, and
yet most people don't take the time to read it."

I then added, "Do you know what the word *Bible* actually stands for?"

Victor inquired, "No, what does it stand for?"

I replied with a playful tone, "Basic Instructions before Leaving
Earth."

He seemed surprised and asked, "Really?"

I chuckled and said, "No, I'm just kidding, but it could be a fitting interpretation."

Taking a more serious tone, I said, "But you know, Victor, like I told you yesterday, you shouldn't worry about what I think about your choice of words, but I do think you should worry about what God thinks because one day you will stand before him—the Creator of the universe—and you will have to give an account for your life."

He responded, "I never looked at it that way before."

I am delighted to share that several months later, I returned to the office in Atlanta for a meeting in the conference room. As I stood at the back of the room, pouring myself a glass of water, a gentle hand touched my shoulder. Turning around, I was met with Victor's warm smile. He said to me, "I just wanted you to know that my wife and I have been attending Bible study classes."

I could not help but respond, "That's fantastic, Victor."

Though Victor and I do not communicate as frequently as we probably should, the last time we have spoken, I can sense a remarkable transformation in him—a man renewed by God's presence in his life. It is evident that he has embraced his faith wholeheartedly and became a true follower of Jesus Christ. Witnessing such positive changes in someone's life is truly heartwarming and a testament to the power of faith and spiritual growth.

○　○　○

Furthermore, there are far too many people who believe they are in good standing with God simply because they attend church a couple of times a month or perform certain daily rituals that make them feel good. Being in right relationship with God has nothing to do with fleeting emotions; it is about the depth and authenticity of our connection with him.

I've attended a nondenominational church in Colorado years ago, and I consider Pastor Matt at that time to be a great teacher. However, like any church, there are aspects with which I may not entirely agree.

Rather than dwell on the specifics, let me share one example that highlights the importance of a genuine relationship with God.

During the worship service, the lead singer sometimes instructs the congregation, just before singing begins and with the music playing, to raise their hands in the air as a way to show God that they want to draw closer to him. Now I have no issue with people who worship in this manner, but I do believe caution is necessary when it comes to this type of worship.

You see, it does not matter how high I raise my hands in the air. I can even venture outside and climb one of the magnificent mountains in Colorado, extending my hands as high as possible, and it will have no bearing on showing God that I desire a closer relationship with him. If I genuinely desire to draw closer to God, then perhaps later that day I will set aside dedicated time to read his Word. But it will not be a mere reading; it will be an in-depth study. There is a significant distinction. It's about having a relationship with God the Father and Jesus, his Son.

Many people read the Word of God solely for information, but we must go beyond that. We should study his Word not for information's sake but to gain knowledge that transforms us. It involves taking what we have read and applying it to our lives. It is akin to someone purchasing a diet book or a book on success. Merely reading it does not put them on a diet or make them successful. True change occurs when they apply what they have learned to their lives. The more they read and apply, the more it begins to alter their actions and behaviors. Those who know them will take notice of the transformation.

That is precisely how we should approach the Word of God. We should read it with the intention of applying its teachings to our lives, becoming the people God intends us to be. This is how we cultivate a genuine relationship with him. Just as buying a diet book does not mean we are on a diet, or reading a book on success does not guarantee success, we are truly on a diet when we begin applying what we have read to our eating habits. Similarly, reading the Word of God is not enough; we must apply its teachings to how we live.

○   ○   ○

Indeed, the book of James offers valuable insight into the importance of not just hearing the Word of God but also actively living it out. In James 1:22–24 (NIV), it states:

> Do not merely listen to the word, and so deceive yourselves. Do what it says. Anyone who listens to the word but does not do what it says is like a man who looks at his face in a mirror and, after looking at himself, goes away and immediately forgets what he looks like.

Consider the scenario of looking into a mirror and noticing something on your face that needs immediate attention. You might think, *How long have I been walking around like this?* The natural response is to wash or correct it. We use a mirror to ensure everything is in order, to identify any necessary corrections or adjustments we need to make to our appearance. James compares this act of self-reflection to reading the Word of God.

When we engage with the Word of God, it serves as a mirror, revealing aspects of our lives that require correction or improvement. It highlights areas where we may fall short or need cleansing. However, if we read the Word of God and fail to apply its teachings to our lives, it is akin to looking in the mirror and recognizing the corrections we need but then walking away and immediately forgetting what we saw.

The Word of God is not meant to be a mere intellectual exercise or a passive activity. It is meant to be lived out, shaping our thoughts, attitudes, and actions. By actively applying the principles and teachings found in scripture, we allow the Word of God to transform us and bring about positive change in our lives. We discover areas that require correction or cleansing, and through obedience and alignment with God's truth, we can experience personal growth and spiritual development.

So let us not be deceived by simply hearing the Word of God without putting it into practice. Instead, let us embrace the mirrorlike nature of scripture, allowing it to reveal the areas where we need correction and actively seeking to align our lives with its teachings.

o   o   o

To this day, my relationship with my ex-wife Terri remains one of genuine friendship and mutual respect. It is remarkable how time and understanding can transform the dynamics of a relationship. Even more heartwarming is the positive connection I share with her husband and daughter. In an unexpected twist of fate, her husband and I have even discovered a shared passion for golf and enjoyed several rounds together. It just goes to show that life has its surprises and silver linings.

Recently, my son, shared an intriguing observation with me. Whenever he tells people that his parents divorced when he was barely two years old, their immediate reaction is usually one of sympathy, followed by the question "Was it hard for you?" Yet to his genuine surprise, he confidently replies, "No, not at all." He explains that our divorce was anything but a bitter separation. Throughout the years, my ex-wife and I have chosen not to allow our personal emotions to cloud our judgment or overshadow the well-being of our child.

Instead, we have made a conscious decision to prioritize our son's happiness and upbringing above all else. Our dedication to him supersedes any past grievances, allowing us to cultivate a peaceful environment for him to grow in. Our conversations and actions are always respectful, ensuring that we never speak negatively about each other in his presence. As a result, he recalls a childhood filled with unity and togetherness, even though we are living separate lives.

In fact, our commitment to amicable coparenting goes beyond the mere necessities. Terri and I remain good friends, and it is not unusual for us to participate in family outings together, creating precious memories that our son still cherishes to this day. It is as though we have found a delicate balance where our affection for his supersedes any personal discord.

Our story teaches us an invaluable lesson—that it is possible to rise above the challenges of divorce and prioritize what truly matters. Our unwavering focus on our son's happiness have allowed us to provide him with a stable and nurturing environment, fostering a strong bond between us and enriching his life.

Divorce can be emotionally charged and challenging, but it does not have to scar the lives of those involved. By placing the needs of our children above all else and fostering an environment of respect and understanding, we can show them that love and family transcend traditional definitions. As a result, even in the face of separation, a harmonious and loving atmosphere can be sustained, leaving a positive impact on the lives of those we hold most dear.

○   ○   ○

When I was around fifteen years old, my father decided to treat the whole family to dinner with his income tax refund. On that evening, my mother instructed us to get ready, and I chose to wear a new T-shirt I had just purchased that did have some inappropriate wording on the front. As I walked into the living room wearing my jeans and T-shirt, my mother immediately objected, telling me to change into another shirt. At the time, I could not understand her reaction and thought she was being rude. After all, I believed it was me who paid for the shirt and my choice.

Now as an adult and a parent myself, I could comprehend the significance behind my mother's request. She was not trying to spoil my day or be mean spirited. Her intention was for me to present myself in a manner that reflected positively on her as a mother. As her child, I was a representation of her, and she did not want me to tarnish that by me wearing an inappropriate shirt. In hindsight, I could empathize with her perspective. She wanted to be proud of me, proud to call me her son.

This parallels our relationship with our heavenly Father. As Christians, our words and actions are a reflection of our identity in Christ. Just as my mother wants me to embody her values and principles, our heavenly Father desires the same. If we claim to be followers of Christ, it is essential to care about our behavior and how we present ourselves before others. Our conduct should bring honor to God and make him proud of us. Similar to the pride God has expressed in his Son when he's proclaimed, "This is my Son, whom I am well pleased," we should strive for him to say the same about us.

Ultimately, there will come a time when we all stand before God. In that moment, we should desire to hear his words of approval, acknowledging our faithfulness and saying, "Well done, my good and faithful servant." Therefore, it is important for us not only to ask ourselves if we truly know Christ but also to consider if he truly knows us (I will explain more about this in chapter five). Our actions should align with our claim of being a follower of Christ, illustrating our authentic relationship with him.

○   ○   ○

An evident relationship with God does not solely rely on external acts such as raising our hands in worship or casually mentioning his name in conversations. True evidence of a relationship with God emerges from a genuine desire to know him more intimately. It is about investing time in getting to know him and earnestly applying his teachings in our lives because we genuinely desire to please him.

To assess our faith and ensure its authenticity, we can ask ourselves some introspective questions. "Has my knowledge of God increased compared with a year ago? Do I hold a deeper reverence for his holiness now than I did before? Am I more awe inspired by his greatness today than I was a year ago? Has my love for him grown and intensified? Do I rely on him more wholeheartedly in all aspects of my life? Is my primary focus centered on pleasing him more than it was a year ago?" These questions serve as self-examination tools to evaluate the authenticity of our faith.

The apostle Paul encourages us to engage in this self-examination in 2 Corinthians 13:5:

> Examine yourselves to see whether you are in the faith;
> test yourselves. Do you not realize that Christ Jesus is in
> you—unless, of course, you fail the test?

He urges us to scrutinize ourselves, to test and evaluate whether we are genuinely walking in faith. He reminds us that Christ Jesus dwells within us, empowering us to live out our faith. By undertaking this examination, we can identify any areas where we may fall short and ensure that our faith remains steadfast and genuine.

In summary, a genuine relationship with God surpasses mere external displays of faith. It begins with a sincere desire to know him more intimately and diligently applying his teachings in our lives. To gauge the authenticity of our faith, we can honestly assess our growth in knowledge, reverence, love, dependence, and devotion to pleasing God. This self-examination aligns with Paul's exhortation to test ourselves and reaffirm our faith in Christ Jesus.

○   ○   ○

The rising number of divorces among Christian marriages can be attributed to the influence of a worldly perspective on marriage. Many Christians have adopted the belief that their happiness should be the foundation of their marital union. When unhappiness arises within the marriage, instead of seeking solutions and working to improve the relationship from within, they look outside the marriage for fulfillment, leading to disastrous consequences. In my own Christian journey, I have observed this mentality portrayed in movies and even heard it expressed by people who use the justification of "God wants me to be happy" when faced with moral dilemmas. However, seeking personal happiness at the expense of God's will is not his desire for us. God's primary desire is for us to be obedient, and through obedience, we find not happiness but true joy.

Joy differs greatly from happiness. Happiness is fleeting and dependent on our circumstances—it comes and goes. If you were to ask long-married couples whether there were times of unhappiness in their marriage, you would overwhelmingly receive a resounding yes. This is because happiness is contingent on external factors. For instance, if I am at my favorite restaurant with beloved friends, savoring my favorite drink, I may feel happy. However, sooner than later, I finish my drink, we leave the restaurant, my friends go their own way, and I am unhappy. Joy, however, is not a by-product of circumstances; it is a profound realization that Jesus is enough in our lives and that I am in good standing with him. Thus, joy can endure even in the face of adversity.

Consider the remarkable example of Paul and Silas in the book of Acts when they were unjustly accused, severely beaten, and imprisoned, their feet bound in stocks.

> The crowd joined in the attack against Paul and Silas. The magistrates ordered them to be stripped and beaten with rods. After they had been severely flogged, they were thrown into prison, and the jailer was commanded to guard them carefully. Upon receiving this order, he put them in the inner cell and fastened their feet in the stocks. Around midnight, Paul and Silas were praying and singing hymns to God, and the other prisoners were listening to them. (Acts 16:22–25, NIV)

Despite the immense suffering they endured, Paul and Silas did not complain or seek pity. Instead, they engaged in prayer and hymns of praise to God, radiating joy even in the darkest of circumstances. Their steadfast faith and unwavering commitment to Christ exemplify the distinction between fleeting happiness and enduring joy.

Therefore, as Christians, we must shift our focus from pursuing fleeting happiness to cultivating a deep-rooted joy that transcends circumstances. Joy stems from an unwavering trust in God's sufficiency and a commitment to obedience. By doing so, we can navigate the challenges of life with resilience, peace, and an unwavering joy that testifies to the transforming power of our faith.

o   o   o

Let us delve into the topic of obedience because it distinguishes itself from mere agreement. Although they may appear similar at times, obedience and agreement are not the same. Allow me to illustrate this with an example.

I learned this lesson from Pastor Carter and saw it come true when my daughter was four years old and ventured close to the street while playing in our front lawn, I would tell her, "Stop, do not go into the street."

Her immediate response would be, "Why, Daddy?"

Then I would explain the dangers of cars driving on the street and how stepping onto it could lead to severe harm. She would nod and say, "OK, Daddy." However, this is not true obedience; it is her considering the situation I have presented and then agreeing with the reasoning behind my instruction. Unfortunately, many Christians today are obedient to God only in matters they agree with.

o o o

Now let us explore another example from the movie *Blast from the Past* that showcases what true obedience entails. In this film, Brendan Fraser portrays the main character who has spent the first thirty-five years of his life starting as a baby living in a fallout shelter. His father has believed a nuclear bomb has exploded, prompting them to seek refuge underground. After thirty-five years, Brendan finally emerges from the shelter and discovers that there has been no bomb. However, he returns to the shelter with a girl named Eve, played by Alicia Silverstone. He informs his parents that he and Eve must go back up for a couple of months but cannot fully explain why. He asks them to lock the doors for two months, assuring them they will return. Perplexed, his father tells him, "But I don't understand."

Brendan then looks at his father with a resolute expression and says, "I am asking you to trust me without understanding why."

Without hesitation, his father replies, "Well, in that case, of course!"

This scene beautifully portrays true obedience—a willingness to trust and follow even without full comprehension. We can gauge our alignment with God's will when we demonstrate obedience without necessarily understanding the reasons behind his commands. It is not about selective agreement but rather a surrendering of our will to God's authority, trusting that his plans are perfect, even if they elude our understanding. True obedience to God requires a humble and steadfast heart, relinquishing the need for complete comprehension and submitting to his guidance.

> We know that we have come to know him if we obey his commands. The man who says, "I know him," but does not do what he commands is a liar, and the truth is not in him. But if anyone obeys his word, God's love is truly made complete in him. This is how we know we are in him: Whoever claims to live in him must walk as Jesus did. (1 John 2:3–6, NIV)

○   ○   ○

Now let us delve back into the issue of abortion. As I've mentioned earlier, if someone claims to be a follower of Christ but believes in pro-choice and finds abortion acceptable, it indicates a lack of true knowledge of God and their unwillingness to obey regardless of their feelings. I am not saying whether that person is saved as I do not know their heart, but I can assert that they do not fully comprehend Christ's perspective on this matter. To support this point, let us turn to the scriptures, specifically the book of Exodus.

Before I do, let us remember the book of Ecclesiastes, which states,

> What has been will be again, what has been done will be done again; there is nothing new under the sun. (Ecclesiastes 1:9, NIV)

in Exodus chapter 1, we encounter the historical account of King Pharaoh, who was the first to implement a form of abortion. Although they did not have the same technology available to us today, the actions taken in that time were the closest equivalent to abortion. During that period, the Israelites were enslaved by the Egyptians for over two hundred years, and King Pharaoh grew concerned as their population began to multiply rapidly. He feared that the Israelites would become strong enough to rebel against their oppressors.

Exodus 1:6–10 (NIV) recounts this situation:

> Now Joseph and all his brothers and all that generation died, but the Israelites were exceedingly fruitful; they multiplied greatly, increased in numbers, and became so numerous that the land was filled with them. Then a new king, who did not know about Joseph, came to power in Egypt. "Look," he said to his people, "the Israelites have become far too numerous for us. Come, we must deal shrewdly with them, or they will become even more numerous, and if a war breaks out, they will join our enemies, fight against us, and leave the country."

Initially, the king attempted to oppress the Israelites through hard labor. However, despite the Egyptians' efforts to suppress them, the Israelites continued to multiply. Consequently, the king resorted to the closest equivalent to abortion as a means to control their population.

Exodus 1:15–16 (NIV) further illustrates the gravity of the situation during that time:

> The king of Egypt said to the Hebrew midwives, whose names were Shiphrah and Puah, "When you are helping the Hebrew women during childbirth on the delivery stool, if you see that the baby is a boy, kill him; but if it is a girl, let her live."

Indeed, this was the closest they could get to abortion given the circumstances. Some might argue that the babies were killed after delivery, but that was primarily due to the technological limitations of that era. If Pharaoh had the means to terminate pregnancies, he would have done so. The king commanded the midwives, who assisted in the childbirth process, to kill any male babies born and deceive others by pretending the child was stillborn. This practice was not uncommon at the time as infant mortality rates were high. Disobeying a king's order during those days carried severe consequences such as imprisonment or death.

However, if we continue reading in verse 17, we discover that the midwives chose not to obey the king's command due to their fear of God:

> The midwives, however, feared God and did not do what the king of Egypt had told them to do; they let the boys live. (Exodus 1:17, NIV)

Their reverence for God and his ways guided their decision, even when they knew that not obeying the king's command could lead to imprisonment or, worse, death. In verse 20, we learn that because of their fear of God, he blessed them, and the Israelite population continued to increase:

> So God was kind to the midwives and the people increased and became even more numerous. And because the midwives feared God, he gave them families of their own (Exodus 1:20-21, NIV)

The midwives' fear of God, which implies deep respect and obedience, resulted in God's favor and blessings on them and the Israelites. This account demonstrates that when we have a genuine relationship with the Creator of the universe, our reverence for him surpasses any fear or obedience to human authority when it comes to his moral law. Pleasing God becomes our priority, even at the cost of our own lives.

o   o   o

This historical example illustrates the issue at hand. It reveals the biblical perspective that regards every human life, including those in the womb, as valuable and worthy of protection. The scripture portrays the act of abortion, even in its historical form, as a response driven by fear and the desire to control a growing population. In fact, there is an organization that exists today that has been originally created for that same purpose. It stands in stark contrast to God's intended purpose for human life and his call to protect and nurture it.

Jesus emphasized a similar perspective in Matthew 10:28 (NIV):

> Do not be afraid of those who kill the body but cannot kill the soul. Rather, be afraid of the One who can destroy both soul and body in hell.

Therefore, as followers of Christ, it is crucial to align our beliefs and actions with the biblical teachings that emphasize the sanctity of life. Abortion, in any form, contradicts this understanding and disregards the inherent value of each person created in the image of God. We should prioritize pleasing him above all else, even if it means going against societal norms or facing persecution. Our fear of God should inspire us to honor his commands and principles, seeking his approval rather than the approval of others.

To any women who may be reading this and have experienced one or more abortions, it is essential to understand a fundamental truth about God's character. When you turn to him in sincere repentance, he is ever forgiving and compassionate. He will not only forgive you completely but also welcome you with open arms, ready to embrace you with his unconditional love. Moreover, God, in his infinite mercy, will not hold your past sins against you; he will remember them no more.

In case you might be wondering about my current wife, around fifteen years after my second divorce, I found myself in a new chapter of life, teaching an adult Sunday school class at Stonebriar Church in

Frisco, Texas. Having made peace with the idea that marriage might not be in my future, I embraced my role as a teacher with contentment. Little did I know that unexpected twists of fate were about to unfold.

After teaching the class for about ten months, one of the associate pastors named Tony approached me with an intriguing proposal. The church was planning to establish a singles class for people in their thirties and forties, and he asked if I would be interested in leading it. Seizing the opportunity, I gladly accepted the responsibility.

On the opening day of the singles class, I stood with Tony and the class administrator at the front, warmly welcoming people as they entered. Coffee and refreshments were available at the back of the room, attracting most attendees. As I watched the group mingling, a thought crossed my mind—could this be God's plan for me to meet someone special?

Among the crowd, a striking woman caught my eye. Her radiant smile immediately captivated me, and I was smitten by her presence. Being the class teacher, I was cautious in my approach, but I made sure to be near her whenever we both reached for our coffee. Her name was Marcey, and I learned she had an identical twin sister, adding an element of fascination to our budding connection.

Months passed, and I mustered the courage to take the next step. I finally asked Marcey to meet for a cup of coffee so that we could continue our conversations, which were often interrupted due to the beginning announcements. Though she claimed I did not technically ask her out on a date but rather for a coffee meetup, it was still a pivotal moment in our journey.

During that first coffee encounter, we both acknowledged our age and the desire for a serious commitment. We delved into conversations that explored potential deal-breakers, laying a strong foundation for what lay ahead. As our connection deepened, I began to realize that Marcey was someone extraordinary—a person I could envision spending the rest of my life with.

Six months later, at the pinnacle of Pikes Peak in Colorado, I got down on one knee and proposed to her. With a breathtaking backdrop and our hearts aligned, she said yes. As if blessing our union, seconds after she said yes, snow started falling for a brief magical moment.

It felt like a sign from above, affirming that God indeed works in mysterious ways.

In the blink of an eye, we went from being two strangers in a Sunday school class to being a couple standing on the precipice of a lifetime together. It was an unexpected and beautiful journey, reminding us that life's twists and turns often lead us to the most unexpected blessings.

CHAPTER 4

KINGDOM MINDED

Death is a subject that many adults tend to avoid and even fear discussing. It is interesting how, despite the inevitability of death, many people live their lives as if they will never face it. However, the truth is that none of us have the power to choose the day we enter or leave this world except in cases of suicide, which I am not referring to here. From the moment we are born, we are destined to eventually pass away.

The discomfort people feel when talking about death often stems from associating it solely with negativity. But for true Christians, death is not something to be feared. It is the moment when God calls them home to spend eternity with him. It is a transition to a glorious existence in his presence. However, for those who do not have a genuine relationship with God, death can be a terrifying prospect. It becomes a time when they will stand before the Creator of the universe and be held accountable for their lives, their sins, and the judgment they will face. It is understandable that discussing a subject that may involve guilt and accountability can be deeply uncomfortable.

It is important to recognize that death is a natural part of life, and for believers, it is the gateway to eternal communion with God. Rather than shying away from the topic, we should approach it with a balanced perspective. By acknowledging the reality of death, we can cultivate a deeper appreciation for the gift of life and make choices that align with our spiritual beliefs. Ultimately, understanding the true significance of death can bring comfort and peace, knowing that for those who have placed their faith in Christ, it is a transition into the presence of a loving and merciful God.

o   o   o

Whenever I am driving in my car and I see a police officer pull up behind me, the first thought that crosses my mind is whether I am adhering to the speed limit. I instinctively check my speed just to be certain. It becomes even more uncomfortable when an officer is behind me on a road where I am unsure of the speed limit. And it is particularly nerve racking when I know I have committed a violation.

There was an incident from about thirty five years ago when I was driving and noticed a police officer pulling up behind me. Suddenly, I remembered an unpaid ticket from a year prior. In that moment, anxiety surged through me, and I made a conscious effort to obey every traffic law meticulously. Desperation set in, and I even attempted to strike a deal with God, promising to pay the outstanding ticket at the earliest opportunity if I could avoid being pulled over. Unfortunately, God does not engage in such bargaining, and the officer had already detected my speeding half a mile back. As soon as I saw his lights flashing, my stomach dropped, and my heart raced with apprehension.

The reason for my panic was clear—I knew I was guilty of an unpaid ticket, which meant there was a warrant for my arrest. I knew where I was headed. That night I found myself in jail. It was an experience that profoundly affected me, and for the following year, I do not think I exceeded the speed limit even once. It is remarkable how a single night in jail can drastically alter one's perspective and behavior.

Sadly, for nonbelievers, there is no second chance when they pass away. There is no opportunity to pray for help or make amends. Once they enter that realm, they find themselves on trial for their lives, and the verdict will inevitably be guilty. However, for authentic followers of Christ, death is simply a time to be with him—a time to go home, and that is something to be embraced and celebrated.

Paul understood this better than anyone else. He did not view death as a negative thing; in fact, he believed that it would be a gain for him. In the book of Philippians, he expressed his perspective:

> For to me, to live is Christ and to die is gain. If I am to go on living in the body, this will mean fruitful labor for me. Yet what shall I choose? I do not know! I am torn between the two: I desire to depart and be with Christ, which is better by far; but it is more necessary for you that I remain in the body. Convinced of this, I know that I will remain, and I will continue with all of you for your progress and joy in the faith, so that through my being with you again your joy in Christ Jesus will overflow on account of me. (Philippians 1:21–26, NIV)

While Paul acknowledged that being with Christ in death would be far better, he understood that the decision was in God's hands. He recognized that God had a purpose for him and that his work was not yet completed.

It is important to note that although death can be a difficult experience for those left behind, having the assurance of where a believer has gone brings comfort. Unfortunately, many Christians still view death negatively because they lack understanding and a mindset focused on the kingdom of God.

○　○　○

Let us remember that God does not determine whether a person is alive by whether their heart is beating. No, he determines whether a person is alive by whether they have eternal life. Eternal life, according to Christ, begins the moment a person is saved. Therefore, it is not something to be associated with negativity as it is a gift and a promise of life with God for eternity.

Jesus has emphasized the significance of belief in him in the book of John:

> Whoever believes in the Son has eternal life, but whoever rejects the Son will not see life, for God's wrath remains on him. (John 3:36, NIV)

According to this verse, eternal life begins when a person believes in Jesus. Therefore, death is merely the transition from our earthly dwelling to being with Christ in his heavenly home.

In 2 Corinthians, Paul also shares his perspective on this matter:

> Therefore we are always confident and know that as long as we are at home in the body we are away from the Lord. For we live by faith, not by sight. We are confident, I say, and would prefer to be away from the body and at home with the Lord. (2 Corinthians 5:6–8, NIV)

Eternal life, as defined by Jesus in John 17:3 (NIV), goes beyond mere duration; it's rooted in a profound relationship. It's the intimate knowledge of the Father and the Son, emphasizing a connection and communion with the divine. This understanding challenges us to prioritize the depth and quality of our relationship with God and Jesus Christ as the essence of eternal life.

○   ○   ○

Many Christians today fear death because they have become too attached to the things of this world. Their worldly-mindedness hinders them from embracing a kingdom-minded perspective where pleasing God takes priority over worldly desires. The Bible encourages us to live as aliens in this world, recognizing that it is not our permanent home but a temporary dwelling. Paul's example teaches us that he not only lacked fear of death but also spoke openly about it. What fueled

Paul's passion for life and enabled him to talk about joy even while imprisoned? It was his focus on the afterlife rather than this present life.

By living with a kingdom-minded perspective and prioritizing our relationship with God, we can overcome the fear of death and find purpose and joy in every day, just as Paul did. Paul had a profound passion, but it was not for the things of this world; his true passion was focused on the ultimate prize, which was the afterlife. This was why he became a follower of Christ. Paul did not embark on his journey as a disciple of Christ hoping for material blessings or an improved earthly life. His decision was driven by the promise of eternal life, and that became his unwavering passion.

○ ○ ○

Speaking of passions, one of my personal favorite sports is hockey. I love attending games or watching them on TV, especially when it involves my hometown team, the Detroit Red Wings. They hold a special place in my heart. While I thoroughly enjoy the game, it is just not the same when the Red Wings are not playing.

On the other hand, my interest in football has waned over time. The game no longer captivates me as it used to, mainly due to the excessive self-centeredness exhibited by many players. The ostentatious showboating and celebratory dances after each successful play have diminished my enjoyment. However, I do catch a game here and there whenever the Cowboys are playing.

In hockey, when a player scores a goal, they pump their fist a couple of times and then promptly head to the bench to high-five their teammates. They understand that it is about the collective effort of the team, not just one individual. I hope this fundamental team spirit never changes in hockey. However, I fear that as time goes on, certain players with an inflated sense of self-importance might enter the NHL and diminish my love for the game.

Hockey also boasts a tradition that has endured for as long as I can remember. Once the playoffs begin, regardless of the intensity of the games or any previous on-ice altercations, when the series concludes, all players from both teams gather at center ice to shake hands and exchange the mutual sentiment of "good game." It is a remarkable display of sportsmanship and respect that adds to the essence of the sport.

o o o

When I was a child, my elder brothers would take me to some of the games in Detroit. Despite not being able to afford tickets, they had connections with older gentlemen who worked at the stadium, allowing us to enter through the back door for free. Although many times we had to watch from the standing-room-only section due to sold-out games, I cherished those moments and could not imagine being anywhere else.

One of my favorite players from recent years and who had now retried was Pavel Datsyuk. I was constantly amazed by his exceptional puck-handling skills while gracefully skating on the ice. In one game, I witnessed him maneuver his way between three opposing players and score a remarkable goal. I was captivated and watched the replay in awe, contemplating the immense passion and drive these players possess every time they step onto the ice.

From the very first game of the season, every team and player on the ice shares a common goal—the Stanley Cup. In hockey, the Stanley Cup is regarded as one of the most prestigious trophies in all sports. Each member of the winning team has the honor of having their names engraved on the cup permanently, and they get the opportunity to spend a day or two with it. The pursuit of the cup fuels the passion of every player throughout each game, extending beyond the immediate match at hand. Whenever the announcers delve into a player's life story during intermissions, there is one recurring theme. Without fail, NHL players express that they have dreamed of having their names inscribed on the Stanley Cup ever since their early days playing on little league teams. The desire to see their name on the cup and to hold it for a day or two remains a constant source of motivation and aspiration.

o o o

In a similar vein, Paul became a follower of Christ, driven by the desire to have his name written in the book of life. He lived each day with a fervent passion as an authentic Christian, keeping a kingdom-minded attitude with his eyes on the ultimate outcome—to be in heaven and united with Christ. David, too, lived his life with this mindset, as expressed in Psalm 27:4 (NIV).

> One thing I ask from the LORD,
> this only do I seek:
> that I may dwell in the house of the LORD
> all the days of my life,
> to gaze on the beauty of the LORD
> and to seek him in his temple.

Living a life that is kingdom-minded entails prioritizing the eternal over the transient things of this world. This principle is underscored by Jesus's teachings in Matthew 6:19–20, where he cautions against storing up earthly treasures that can be destroyed or stolen. Instead, he urges us to accumulate treasures in heaven, where they remain secure and unaffected by earthly decay or theft.

To grasp the context of this message, Jesus advises us not to perform acts seeking the praise of others, for if we receive their recognition, that becomes our sole reward. Rather, our actions should be directed toward pleasing God, not seeking approval from others.

Let me illustrate this with an example. When my son was five years old and playing flag football, his sole focus was catching my attention. After making a remarkable play, his primary concern was coming to me and asking, "Did you see that?" Living a life that is kingdom-minded implies that our primary aim is to please God and align ourselves with his agenda.

This is why, as mentioned earlier, God does not merely request but rather commands us to be men and women of courage. Scriptures such as the following emphasize the call to be strong and courageous, assuring us that the Lord is with us, never forsaking us or leaving us:

Be strong and courageous. Do not be afraid or terrified because of them, for the LORD your God goes with you; he will never leave you nor forsake you. (Deuteronomy 31:6, NIV)

Have I not commanded you? Be strong and courageous. Do not be afraid; do not be discouraged, for the LORD your God will be with you wherever you go. (Joshua 1:9, NIV)

Be on your guard; stand firm in the faith; be courageous; be strong. (1 Corinthians 16:13, NIV)

When our desire is to please God, even if it means going against the tide of the world, we will require courage to stand firm. G. K. Chesterton has aptly described *courage* as "a strong desire to live, while taking the form of a readiness to die." Living in a society like America, courage may not always seem necessary, but the times are changing rapidly.

In various parts of the world, many Christians exhibit unwavering strength even in the face of imminent execution. These people truly comprehend the essence of standing firm and exemplify courage in its purest form.

o   o   o

Throughout my years as a follower of Christ, I had faced persecution for my faith only once, and even then, it was a mild form of persecution through words. I used to visit a client regularly who had been a significant source of business for the company I worked for. This particular visit followed the usual monthly routine. The owner, who was of Jewish faith, sat at his desk while I stood in his office. He began asking me questions about my faith and then stated his perception that Christians have a middleman to go through, whereas Jews can approach God directly. I tried explaining that Jesus is God and his sacrifice on the cross allows us to approach God without any blemish. He then asked about tithing, and upon hearing that I tithe 10 percent, he burst into laughter, claiming that my religion had brainwashed me. He called his secretary into the office and shared his belief that I was involved in a cult, attempting to provoke laughter. However, I could sense the secretary's pity for me through her eyes. In that moment, I started to smile, but I did not reveal the reason behind it. Despite his mocking, I remembered a verse from Jesus.

> Blessed are you when people insult you, persecute you, and falsely say all kinds of evil against you because of me. Rejoice and be glad, because great is your reward in heaven, for in the same way, they persecuted the prophets who were before you. (Matthew 5:11–12, NIV)

The key to remaining strong and courageous is to remember God's promises. While my experience was a mild form of persecution, it becomes even more challenging for those who risk their lives for their faith. However, I can assure you that those who endure true persecution also hold on to God's promises.

A powerful example of this can be seen in a video called "Sheep among Wolves," which I highly recommend watching. It portrays the underground church rapidly growing in Iran, led by women. In an interview, two women shares their experiences, and one of them admits living in constant fear, never knowing when the Iranian police may raid her home. She understands the consequences if exposed: she will be raped in front of her husband, he will be killed, and she will eventually be killed or imprisoned. When asked how she copes with this, she quotes Romans 12:1 (NIV):

> Therefore, I urge you, brothers and sisters, in view of God's mercy, to offer your bodies as a living sacrifice, holy and pleasing to God—this is your true and proper worship.

To possess such a mindset is truly to adopt a kingdom-minded perspective.

○ ○ ○

When our focus shifts to the kingdom, we become driven to fulfill Jesus's final commandment: sharing the Gospel and making Disciples. If you find yourself not actively spreading the Good News, it usually stems from not truly being amazed by His grace. This could be due to not fully embracing your identity as a profound sinner. While you acknowledge your imperfections, you might not perceive them as deeply alarming compared to notorious criminals. But it is crucial to understand that, without Christ, our trajectory was no different from history's darkest figures, heading toward the same inevitable destination.

When we become truly amazed at who God is and what Jesus has done for us, it naturally compels us to share, even against a strong warning from Jesus himself. To illustrate, consider this incident found in Mark:

A man with leprosy came to him and begged him on his knees, "If you are willing, you can make me clean."

Jesus was indignant. He reached out his hand and touched the man. "I am willing," he said. "Be clean!" Immediately the leprosy left him and he was cleansed.

Jesus sent him away at once with a strong warning: "See that you don't tell this to anyone. But go, show yourself to the priest and offer the sacrifices that Moses commanded for your cleansing, as a testimony to them." Instead he went out and began to talk freely, spreading the news. As a result, Jesus could no longer enter a town openly but stayed outside in lonely places. Yet the people still came to him from everywhere. (Mark 1: 40-45 (NIV)

Similarly, our former state was marked by spiritual affliction and estrangement. Yet, through Jesus' amazing grace, we are adopted as

God's beloved children and cleansed by His sacrificial blood. When we truly grasp what Jesus has done for us, we too cannot help to share with others.

In Mark 7, we witness how people defied Jesus's instruction not to spread the news, and in verse thirty-seven we learn why.

People were overwhelmed with amazement. (NIV)

There's a powerful scene in the movie "The Green Mile," Paul (Tom Hanks) grapples with his conscience. Entrusted with overseeing the execution of John Coffey, a man he knows to be innocent and blessed with a divine gift of healing, Paul confronts the weight of potential damnation. As he sits in contemplation, Paul shares his inner turmoil with his wife, acknowledging, "I have done some things in my life that I am not proud of, but this is the first time I ever felt real danger of hell." Despite his internal conflict, his wife encourages him to talk to John Coffey.

The following day, Paul enters John's cell, pulls up a small bench, and takes a seat to engage in a crucial conversation. He begins, "John, I have to ask you something very important now." Anticipating Paul's query, John interjects, "I know what you're going to say, and you don't have to say it." However, Paul insists, "No, I do," and asks John, "do you want me to let you go and see how far you can get?" In response, John says, "Why would you do a foolish thing like that?" Paul, wearing a grave expression, answers, "On the day of my judgment, when I stand before God, and he asks me, why did you kill one of his true miracles? What am I going to say, that it was my job." Repeating this justification, Paul's solemn demeanor reveals his awareness that such an excuse will not suffice in the eyes of God. However, John provides a comforting response.

This poignant cinematic moment serves as a metaphor, prompting reflection on our own actions. When God questions why we did not share the gospel more fervently, what are we going to say? That life got too busy and we didn't have the time. We need to dive deeper in our relationship with God so that we can become more amazed at who he is and what Jesus did for us. It not, we too will find ourselves in Paul shoes at the end of our life, knowing that such an excuse will not suffice in the eyes of God.

o   o   o

During my teenage years, I sat in the living room with my parents and siblings, watching the news unfold on the television. There was a reporter who had been granted permission to board a plane that had been hijacked by a group known as the PLO. The interviewer had a conversation with one of the hijackers who was in charge, and she asked him a poignant question: "Aren't you afraid to die, knowing that there are soldiers outside this plane ready to shoot you?" In response, he gazed at her with a solemn expression and uttered, "I died the minute I joined the PLO." That profound statement became etched in my memory, and it mirrored the essence of being a follower of Christ with a kingdom-minded perspective.

The moment we embrace Christianity, just like that hijacker, we undergo a spiritual death to our old selves, and we embark on a new life wholly dedicated to pleasing God. This is why Jesus has emphasized the necessity of being born again to enter the kingdom of God.

In today's world, many people make career choices based on the benefits they offer, such as a company's 401(k) plan. They understand that a job with good benefits and a solid retirement plan holds greater value in the long run, even if the initial pay may be less. The payoff in the end outweighs the salary reduction they may have taken years ago.

I often liken Christianity to a job. It can be a challenging job since it goes against the ways of the world, and the monetary rewards may not be extravagant. However, the benefits and the eternal plan of salvation are beyond compared. It prompts us to introspect and ask ourselves, "What are we truly seeking? Are we pursuing worldly comforts and temporary possessions, or are we seeking a kingdom minded perspective?"

o   o   o

As you know, at eighteen, I enlisted in the army and became a military police officer. However, what you do not know is for the first year and a half, I was stationed at Fort Meade, Maryland, where they had two MP platoons that took turns rotating duties each month. One month one platoon would handle patrol duty, patrolling the military base in our MP vehicles, while the other platoon would focus on war games. During the war games month, we would spend one to two weeks in the woods, simulating actual warfare scenarios.

On a particular month, we found ourselves facing the formidable Eighty-Second Airborne Division. They demonstrated their prowess by parachuting in one night, catching us off guard. I would like to tell you that we held our ground, but that would not be true. Needless to say, they defeated us in a mere three days.

After the intense war activity came to an end on a Friday, we returned to the barracks the next morning to unpack and clean up. That night some of us decided to head out to the local bar for a couple of drinks. As fate would have it, when we entered the bar, we encountered about four soldiers from the Eighty-Second Division. Unable to resist some friendly banter about why we lost, we engaged in good-natured trash talk with them.

After around twenty minutes of back-and-forth, one of the soldiers from the Eighty-Second Division proposed a challenge to determine who was tougher. The rules were simple but intense: One of their soldiers and one of ours would place their arms on the table, with their arms rubbing against each other from wrist to elbow. A lit cigarette would then be placed between their arms; then the two soldiers would slowly roll up the arms pressing against the cigarette, putting it out. If neither soldier would surrender, then another cigarette was lit, and the process would repeat until someone gave in.

We agreed to the challenge, with our team winning the first round and their taking the second and third rounds. I was the last one to participate, but it was a good thing because, by then, I had several drinks, and the alcohol in my system had given me some confidence, and I was determined not to give in easily.

When it was my turn, I placed my arm down on the table next to his, and he lit the cigarette, making it glow bright red. As we rolled up our arms together, the pain was undeniable, but I refused to flinch. After a couple of cigarettes, I decided to try a different tactic. I picked up the cigarette, took two big puffs (I did not inhale because I was not a smoker), looked him in the eye, and put the lit tip on my arm, rotating it back and forth as I pressed down as if my arm were an ashtray. You could smell the stench from my burning skin. I relit the cigarette, took two more puffs, and handed it back to him. He paused for a moment, then conceded, saying, "You win."

I felt victorious, and we were all happy with the tie. However, the next morning brought a different story. My arm was far worse than I had anticipated, and I did not feel so victorious about my bold move.

I wasted no time and rushed to the hospital for medical attention. After waiting anxiously for about ten minutes in the examination room, a doctor walked in; I quickly noticed that he was a captain. He looked at my arm and inquired about the incident. The truth was evident from the state of my arm, so I openly shared what had transpired. Without hesitation, he left the room, and moments later, a stern-looking colonel doctor entered.

He sternly warned me that I could be charged with damage to government property, which would jeopardize any chances of promotion and keep me as a private first class for years. He emphasized, "You do not belong to yourself anymore; you belong to the United States Army. Do you understand me, Private?"

I immediately replied with "Yes, sir."

Those words—you do not belong to yourself anymore—marked a turning point in my military career. It made me realize that my life was no longer my own; I belonged to the US Army, whether I wore the uniform or not. This newfound sense of responsibility prompted me to take my role more seriously. Just before my third year, I was recommended for the position of sergeant.

○   ○   ○

I share this story because it closely parallels the Christian journey. Before we come to Christ, we have all belonged to Satan, but through the redemptive work of Jesus, we have been bought with a price—the precious blood of Christ. Paul eloquently expresses this truth in 1 Corinthians 6:12–20 (NIV).

> "I have the right to do anything," you say—but not everything is beneficial. "I have the right to do anything"—but I will not be mastered by anything. You say, "Food for the stomach and the stomach for food, and God will destroy them both." The body, however, is not meant for sexual immorality but for the Lord, and the Lord for the body. By his power God raised the Lord from the dead, and he will raise us also. Do you not know that your bodies are members of Christ himself? Shall I then take the members of Christ and unite them with a prostitute? Never! Do you not know that he who unites himself with a prostitute is one with her in body? For it is said, "The two will become one flesh." But whoever is united with the Lord is one with him in spirit.
>
> Flee from sexual immorality. All other sins a person commits are outside the body, but whoever sins sexually, sins against their own body. Do you not know that your bodies are temples of the Holy Spirit, who is in you, whom you have received from God? You are not your own; you were bought at a price. Therefore honor God with your bodies.

Understanding this profound truth shifts our perspective and motivates us to live in a manner worthy of our new identity. Just as I took my military role more seriously after realizing I belonged to the US Army, acknowledging that our identity is in Christ compels us to honor him in all aspects of life. Living with a kingdom-minded spirit means seeking first his kingdom, aligning our thoughts and actions with his will, and pursuing righteousness.

As Christians, we no longer walk in the old ways but strive to be living testimonies of God's grace and love. We are called to walk in obedience, serving others, and spreading the message of the Gospel. Our lives should reflect the transformation that has taken place within us, allowing his light to shine through us and drawing others closer to him.

In conclusion, living with a kingdom-minded spirit means embracing our new identity in Christ, recognizing that we are no longer our own but his beloved children. This realization empowers us to live a life that glorifies God, honoring him with every thought, word, and action. Let us be motivated by the love he has poured into our lives and share that love with the world around us.

○　○　○

Many years ago, I had the privilege of attending and teaching in a remarkable Bible study class called BSF (Bible Study Fellowship), which I attended for thirteen years; twelve of those years I was a children's leader. During our study of Moses, there were some people who found it difficult to accept that Moses did not get to see the Promised Land due to one seemingly small mistake. For those unfamiliar with Moses's story, allow me to provide some context.

Moses spent the first forty years of his life believing he was a great leader and hoping that God would use him to free his people from slavery. However, God had a different plan for Moses. He wanted to instill humility in him before entrusting him with such a significant mission. So Moses spent the following forty years of his life thinking he was a nobody, unaware that God was preparing him for the task of delivering his people.

At the age of eighty, God finally called on Moses to lead the Israelites out of Egypt and into the Promised Land. Moses experienced the awe-inspiring events of the ten plagues and successfully confronted Pharaoh, leading to the liberation of his people from slavery. Nevertheless, he then faced the challenge of guiding the Israelites through the wilderness for forty years, enduring their constant grumbling and complaints.

○　○　○

After nearly thirty-seven years of wandering in the desert, Moses made a mistake by not following God's instructions precisely. As a consequence, God informed Moses that he would not be allowed to enter the Promised Land as a result of his transgression.

The question arises: was God fair in denying Moses entry into the Promised Land due to his sin? The answer is a resounding yes. We must remember that God is perfect and holy, and even a single sin is enough to render us guilty and unfit to enter the kingdom of heaven. This serves as a powerful reminder of our need for God's grace, which he abundantly provides through his Son, Jesus Christ.

Now it is important to recognize that Moses had a unique and intimate relationship with God that set him apart from anyone else. He was chosen by God to fulfill a significant role in the history of his people. Moses was not only a leader and a deliverer but also a friend of God. The scriptures tell us that Moses spoke to God face-to-face as one would speak to a friend.

This special relationship with God highlights the depth of God's love and favor toward Moses. Despite Moses's shortcomings and the consequences he faced, God's grace and presence remained with him throughout his journey. It serves as a testament to the faithfulness of God, who remains steadfast even in the face of human weakness and sin.

○   ○   ○

Moses's profound story serves as a powerful reminder that, as believers, we are not immune to the influence of sin and its repercussions. It is crucial to understand that while the consequences a believer faces for their mistakes are not eternal, they can still have earthly implications. In Moses's case, though he could not enter the Promised Land on the earth due to his actions, he ultimately inherited the eternal Promised Land.

This teaches us a valuable lesson about the nature of God's forgiveness and grace. Even though we may stumble and face temporal consequences for our wrongs, God's love and mercy are ever present. Our shortcomings do not define our eternal destiny as God offers us the hope of redemption and a place in his eternal kingdom.

Moses's unwavering acceptance of God's decision regarding his entry into the Promised Land could be attributed to his transformed goals and priorities. His relationship with God and his dedication to the Israelites took precedence over personal desires. When the Israelites sinned and faced God's wrath, Moses interceded on their behalf, pleading with God not to destroy them. His focus was on pleasing God and ensuring the welfare of the people, rather than on his own ambitions.

o　o　o

This stands in stark contrast to the story Jesus shares in Luke 12:16–21(NIV) through a parable. It revolves around a man whose aspirations and pursuits are solely centered on worldly matters rather than eternal ones. The parable illustrates the dangers of placing one's ultimate goal and fulfillment in temporal possessions and earthly achievements.

> The ground of a certain rich man yielded an abundant harvest. He thought to himself, "What shall I do? I have no place to store my crops."
>
> Then he said, "This is what I'll do. I will tear down my barns and build bigger ones, and there I will store my surplus grain. And I'll say to myself, 'You have plenty of grain laid up for many years. Take life easy; eat, drink and be merry.'"
>
> But God said to him, "You fool! This very night your life will be demanded from you. Then who will get what you have prepared for yourself?"
>
> This is how it will be with whoever stores up things for themselves but is not rich toward God.

This parable serves as a poignant reminder for us to examine our own priorities and goals. Are we consumed by the temporary pleasures and treasures of this world, or do we seek after the eternal riches found in a relationship with God? It urges us to align our aspirations with those that have eternal significance and to prioritize our relationship with God above all else.

○ ○ ○

It is crucial to recognize that when we prioritize worldly goals above seeking God's kingdom, we risk being called fools by God himself. Why is this the case? Because none of us know the exact moment when we will depart from this world and stand before him in judgment. Living as if we will exist indefinitely, solely focused on worldly achievements, is a foolish and misguided approach. To be unprepared to stand before God is the epitome of foolishness.

God's perspective differs greatly from the world's standards. Possessing impressive degrees, accumulating vast wealth, or achieving worldly success holds no weight in God's eyes if they are pursued at the expense of neglecting our relationship with him. A fool, according to God, is someone who lacks true knowledge, someone who places their hope and trust in earthly matters before him.

○ ○ ○

Please understand that setting goals and pursuing success in earthly endeavors is not inherently wrong. However, when those goals become our primary focus, there is a significant risk of disappointment when circumstances fail to align with our desires. Placing the pursuit of worldly achievements above seeking God's kingdom leaves us vulnerable to disillusionment and emptiness.

Rather than being labeled as fools by God, we should strive to align our priorities with his eternal truth. Our main goal should be to seek God, to know him intimately, and to live according to his will. When we make a genuine relationship with God our priority, our perspective on worldly achievements and material possessions undergoes a transformative shift.

Ultimately, it is in seeking God's kingdom that we find true fulfillment and lasting treasures. We are called to prioritize eternal values over temporary pursuits, investing in the things that have everlasting significance. By aligning our goals with God's purposes, we can avoid the label of foolishness and live with purpose, knowing that our ultimate destiny lies in his hands.

○   ○   ○

Let us therefore seek wisdom, seek the truth, and seek the kingdom of God above all else. In doing so, we will avoid the folly of worldly pursuits and embrace a life that is grounded in the eternal perspective of God's kingdom. That is why Jesus says in Matthew 6:31 (NIV):

> So do not worry, saying, "What shall we eat?" or "What shall we drink?" or "What shall we wear?" For the pagans run after all these things, and your heavenly Father knows that you need them. But seek first his kingdom and his righteousness, and all these things will be given to you as well. Therefore do not worry about tomorrow, for tomorrow will worry about itself. Each day has enough trouble of its own.

Jesus, in his teachings, emphasizes the importance of prioritizing God's kingdom and righteousness above worldly concerns. In the book of Matthew, he reminds us not to worry about our basic needs such as food, drink, or clothing. He contrasts the behavior of pagans who relentlessly pursue these temporal things with the instructions he gives to his followers.

Jesus assures us that our heavenly Father is fully aware of our needs. Instead of being consumed by anxiety over worldly matters, we are encouraged to seek first God's kingdom and his righteousness. By making God the priority of our lives, aligning our hearts and actions with his will, we can trust that our needs will be provided for.

This does not mean that we neglect our responsibilities or become apathetic toward our daily needs. Rather, it is an invitation to reorient our hearts and minds, recognizing that God's kingdom and righteousness should hold supreme importance in our lives. When we prioritize our relationship with God and live according to his principles, he promises to take care of our needs.

Jesus reminds us not to worry excessively about tomorrow, for each day brings its own challenges. By focusing on the present moment and entrusting our future to God, we can experience freedom from the burden of anxiety. Our confidence lies in knowing that our heavenly Father, who lovingly cares for us, will provide what is necessary.

○   ○   ○

One of the most cherished memories I hold of my mother is her passing, a memory that fills my heart with joy every time I reflect on it. She was a deeply devoted Catholic, and her two brothers had dedicated their lives as Catholic priests in a church in Mexico and then became bishops. Throughout the years, I endeavored to help my mother grasp the truths revealed in scripture. However, whenever I presented her with passages that challenged her beliefs, she would seek solace by consulting her brothers, who always reassured her that she was in good standing with God. They would tell her what she wanted to hear, providing a sense of comfort and affirmation.

Years ago, my mother received a cancer diagnosis. The doctors informed her that radiation treatment was her only option, cautioning that due to her age, the procedure would be arduous and may not completely eliminate the cancer. Recognizing that her time on the earth may be drawing to a close, she made the decision to forgo radiation treatment and instead spend her remaining months at home with her family.

About six months before her passing, I visited her at home. She resided with my elder sister, Sonia, and my elder brother Sam. During that visit, my mother asked me to read a small book sent to her by one of her bishop brothers titled *How a Catholic May Know If They're Going to Heaven*. Initially, I felt hesitant, skeptical that the book might simply offer comforting words without biblical foundation. However, honoring my mother's request, I agreed to read it, making a pact with her. I would cross-reference each scriptural reference, and if I discovered any misquotations, I would cease reading.

Leaving the kitchen to fetch my Bible from the car, I returned, prepared to examine the book closely. As I delved into its contents, scrutinizing each passage alongside the corresponding biblical verses, I found myself astonished. The book eloquently and accurately expounded on the scriptural truth that salvation comes solely through faith in Jesus Christ rather than through good works or religious rituals.

With every turn of the page, my heart resonated with the book's teachings as it clarified misconceptions that had plagued my mother's faith journey for years. It emphasized the necessity of repentance, turning to Christ, and accepting his forgiveness. The importance of cultivating a personal relationship with Jesus, surrendering our lives to him as Lord and Savior, was underscored.

o   o   o

I soon discovered that the book was written by a man whose wife was diagnosed with cancer, prompting her to ask a profound question: "How can I be certain of my salvation, and what about purgatory?" Deeply concerned for his wife's spiritual well-being, the husband embarked on a determined quest to find the answers. He delved into the pages of the Bible, spending countless hours in search of clarity.

Despite his dedicated research, he found no mention of purgatory within the biblical text. Recognizing his own limited knowledge of the scriptures, he turned to his church, seeking guidance from a priest who might shed light on the subject. However, to his disappointment, the priest was unable to provide a single verse referencing purgatory.

Driven by a thirst for understanding, the husband immersed himself in the study of Catholic history. Through his diligent exploration, he unearthed the origins of the concept of purgatory, realizing that it was an invention of the church established many centuries ago for profit. In summary, the book was penned by a man who discovered the truth about what scripture truly communicates regarding reconciliation with God.

After I had finished reading the book, I turned to my mother and asked her directly, "Did you read this book?"

Her expression revealed surprise and being caught off guard, and she replied, "No!"

Sensing the discrepancy, I continued, saying, "Mom, I don't think your brother even read it. There is no way he would have sent it if he had read it himself. He probably just saw the title and assumed it would be fitting for you."

With a sense of gratitude, I added, "Next time you speak to your brother, please convey my heartfelt thanks for sending you this book."

From that day forward, I could perceive that my mother had numerous questions stirring within her. However, her pride prevented her from openly seeking answers.

o   o   o

About a month later, during another visit to my mother's house, she approached me with a question. "Danny," she began, "can I ask you something?"

I assured her that she could, and she continued, "You know my sister in Mexico, the one going through a difficult time? Last week, she went without food for two days because she does not have any money. You know I give money to the church every month, right?" I confirmed my awareness of her regular donations.

She hesitated for a moment and then asked, "Would it be OK if I took some of the money I give to the church and gave it to my sister?"

Without hesitation, I responded, "Absolutely, Mom. That's what the money is for—to help build God's kingdom and assist those in need." Curiosity piqued, I inquired further, asking why she was seeking my opinion.

She explained, "Well, I called one of my brothers and asked him if it would be OK to use the church money for my sister, and he said no! He insisted it was God's money. But when I called my other brother, he said yes. I'm just confused."

Reflecting on her statement, I realized she had two brothers who had devoted their lives as priests/bishops to the Catholic Church, yet they provided conflicting answers to the same question. I gently suggested, "Mom, don't you think it's time for you to explore what the Bible has to say for yourself?"

After contemplating my words for a few moments, my mother's expression turned to one of confusion. She looked at me and said, "If you want to start coming over to the house for a Bible study, I will join you."

Filled with joy, I responded, "That's great, Mom! I'll come over once a week, and we can study the Bible together."

A smile graced her face as she replied, "OK."

A few days later, with my Bible in hand, I arrived at my mother's house for our scheduled Bible study. To my surprise, my brother and sister expressed their interest in joining us. My sister Sonia was somewhat considered the black sheep of the family at that time. She had no knowledge of scripture and had never shown any desire to learn. Running her business from home, she had developed a reputation for being dishonest, saying and doing whatever it took to make money.

o   o   o

Knowing that my mother had limited time left, I decided to take a quick journey through the Old Testament during our study. My intention was not to frighten her but rather to help her understand the righteous anger of God. I believed that when people recognize their own sinful nature and grasp the just nature of God, they develop a deeper appreciation for his grace. Many churches emphasize God's love while neglecting to address his wrath. As a result, instead of acknowledging our desperate need for God's grace, we begin to perceive his grace as something we deserve.

This distorted perception often leads Christians to justify their own sins. It is a symptom of the prevalent lack of fear of God among many believers today. Even Christians fail to recognize the severity of their own sinfulness. When they evaluate their lives, they believe that

God must be pleased with them simply because they attend church and profess to be Christians. However, if a person fails to grasp their true need, they cannot fully comprehend or appreciate what they truly need. It was only when I fully understood my own desperation that I began to truly appreciate the significance of Christ's sacrifice on the cross for me.

Despite her initial skepticism, my mother remained cautious during our Bible study sessions. Every time I read a Bible verse, she would pause and say, "Wait, wait a minute," following along in her own Bible to ensure I was not fabricating anything. Her Bible was an enormous tome, measuring about a foot and a half long and wide, twice the size of the yellow pages, complete with pictures. It had remained mostly untouched over the years, and its pages were still crisp.

After a few weeks of delving into the Old Testament and witnessing God's righteous disdain for sin and his wrath, something unexpected occurred. My sister Sonia suddenly interjected, saying, "Danny, this is all amazing, and I'm enjoying it, but I need to know now: how does a person get saved?" We halted our study right there, and I shared the Gospel with her. That very night, she accepted Christ.

o   o   o

Around two months later, my mother's condition worsened as the cancer progressed, causing her to sleep extensively during the day. Throughout the week, I would call the house to check on her, and either my brother or sister would inform me of her diminishing strength and prolonged sleep. There were occasions when my brother answered the phone and conveyed that our mother had emerged from her room into the kitchen, wearing a sad expression. However, upon seeing my brother Sam, she would beam with a big smile and ask him, "Sam, is Danny coming over today for a Bible study?"

Sadly, my brother had to respond, "No, Mom, not today." He admitted feeling saddened when he had to deliver the news because, upon hearing it, she would simply lower her head and retreat back to her room.

Recognizing my mother's genuine enjoyment of our Bible studies and her deteriorating physical state, I made the decision to increase our study sessions to several times a week. When I informed her of my plan, she was ecstatic with excitement.

○   ○   ○

About a week later, my mother developed pneumonia and had to be hospitalized for a few days. During one of my visits, as I entered her room, I noticed her praying with her rosary in hand. Not wanting to interrupt her, I quietly decided to take a walk around the hospital. When I returned, I entered her room to find her putting away the rosary. She asked me when I had arrived, and I replied, "I've been here for about fifteen minutes, but I noticed you were praying, so I went for a walk."

With a smile on her face, she looked at me and said, "Danny, what does the Bible have to say about the rosary?"

Pausing for a moment, I carefully considered my response. "Well," I began, "do you want to know the truth or something that will make you feel good?"

Without hesitation, she replied, "The truth, of course."

Gathering my thoughts, I explained, "Mom, the truth is that the Bible doesn't mention the rosary. It does not specifically talk about that practice. While prayer is indeed discussed in the Bible, the rosary itself is something that the Catholic Church established many years ago."

Her voice filled with anger, she retorted, "What do you mean the Catholic Church came up with it?"

Sensing her frustration, I reassured her, "Mom, I'm simply stating that the Bible doesn't mention the rosary specifically. However, if you want to know what Jesus has to say about prayer, I can share that with you."

Her face lit up, and she exclaimed, "Yes, I do!"

With that, I informed her that I would retrieve my Bible from my car and return to read to her what Jesus had to say about prayer. Once

I had the Bible in hand, I opened it to the book of Matthew and began to read aloud.

> And when you pray, do not be like the hypocrites, for they love to pray standing in the synagogues and on the street corners to be seen by men. I tell you the truth, they have received their reward in full. [I explained to her here that if you are seeking the praise of men when doing a good deed, that is your reward, there is not reward in heaven.] But when you pray, go into your room, close the door and pray to your Father, who is unseen. Then your Father, who sees what is done in secret, will reward you. And when you pray, do not keep on babbling like pagans, for they think they will be heard because of their many words. Do not be like them, for your Father knows what you need before you ask him. (Matthew 6:5–13, NIV)

Continuing our conversation, I posed a question to my mother. "When you pray the same prayer over and over, don't you think it's like babbling? After reading what Jesus said about prayer, don't you think you are doing exactly what he advised us not to do?" I gently explained, "Mom, God desires to hear your prayers from the depths of your heart. He wants you to have a genuine conversation with him, not simply repeat words in the belief that you're doing a good job because you've said numerous Our Fathers and Hail Marys."

In that moment, I could see a newfound love for Jesus blossoming within my mother. She developed a deep affection for him, and when she left the hospital, it seemed that she left her rosary behind as well. None of us in the family ever saw it again. It appeared that her focus shifted from religious rituals to a personal heartfelt connection with Jesus.

○   ○   ○

During my mother's last few weeks on the earth, her desire to continue our Bible studies remained unwavering despite her weakening condition. There was only one occasion when she lacked the strength to partake in our study. One Wednesday afternoon, I visited my mother without the intention of conducting a Bible study; I could sense that her time was running short. As she lay in bed, I knelt before her asked, "Mom, with all the knowledge you now have from the Bible, have you invited Christ into your life yet?"

She paused for a few seconds, her face reflecting concern, and replied, "No."

Sensing the urgency, I gently urged her, "Don't you think you should pray and ask him into your heart to receive the gift he offers?"

Her expression turned desperate as she responded, "Yes." Then she made a heartfelt request. "Danny, will you pray with me?"

I reassured her, "Of course, Mom. That's what I was planning on doing." Together, we prayed, and she invited Christ into her life.

After we finished praying, I prepared to leave the room, and she said, "Danny, can we do it again tomorrow?" My heart was lifted with joy.

o o o

When I returned to town on Friday, I called my sister to check on my mother's condition, and she informed me that it was not good. I went to visit her that night, but she could only stay awake for about ten minutes due to the pain medication she was taking. The following day, I visited her again, but this time she did not recognize any of us. She would wake up for brief periods of fifteen minutes every other hour, but she was disoriented.

Realizing that my mother only had a day or two left, we decided to contact our eldest brother, Manuel, who lived in Frisco, Texas, to inform him of the situation. He and his entire family promptly packed their bags and headed for Katy, where my mother resided.

o o o

At around seven o'clock that evening, something remarkable happened. My mother woke up and, for some inexplicable reason, was filled with a newfound burst of energy. With her own strength, she sat up on her bed and looked at Amanda (my niece), expressing her joy at seeing her. As the rest of us entered the room, she recognized each of us and smiled, expressing her happiness to have us all there. We were all taken aback by this sudden change as, just earlier that day, she had been unable to lift herself or recognize anyone.

With everyone gathered around her, I knelt down on one knee in front of her and asked, "Mom, is there anything you want?"

She shook her head and replied, "No." Despite her frail condition, she appeared to be in a remarkably good mood.

Taking note of her demeanor, I jokingly asked, "Mom, do you want us to take you to play bingo?" With a broad smile on her face, she shook her head again and said no.

Then my sister Sandra suggested, "Mom, would you like to do a Bible study?"

In response, my mother raised her head with an even wider smile and said, "Yes." It was evident that she had been contemplating what activity to engage in. So we gathered a couple of Bibles, and the entire family sat around my mother's bed to begin a Bible study session.

I asked my mother if there was any particular passage she wanted us to read. She looked at us and replied, "Not really. You pick."

My sister turned to me and suggested that I read the part when Jesus was on the cross and told the man on the neighboring cross, "Today I will see you in the kingdom of heaven." It seemed like the perfect choice, so we all turned to the book of Luke and began reading those verses.

> Two other men, both criminals, were also led out with him to be executed. When they came to the place called the Skull, there they crucified him, along with the criminals—one on his right, the other on his left. Jesus said, "Father, forgive them, for they do not know what they are doing." And they divided up his clothes by casting lots.

The people stood watching, and the rulers even sneered at him. They said, "He saved others; let him save himself if he is the Christ of God, the Chosen One."

The soldiers also came up and mocked him. They offered him wine vinegar and said, "If you are the king of the Jews, save yourself."

There was a written notice above him, which read: THIS IS THE KING OF THE JEWS.

One of the criminals who hung there hurled insults at him: "Aren't you the Christ? Save yourself and us!"

But the other criminal rebuked him. "Don't you fear God," he said, "since you are under the same sentence? We are punished justly, for we are getting what our deeds deserve. But this man has done nothing wrong."

Then he said, "Jesus, remember me when you come into your kingdom."

Jesus answered him, "I tell you the truth, today you will be with me in paradise." (Luke 23:32–43, NIV)

For the next twenty minutes or more, my mother remained fully engaged in the Bible study. She listened attentively and even participated by asking some questions, just as she had done in previous sessions. Throughout the study, she exuded an incredible sense of peace, and her thoughts were clear and coherent. After we had finished, she looked at all of us and expressed in a very soft voice, "I'm very tired now. Is it OK if I take a nap?" We reassured her that it was perfectly fine, and we left the room to allow her to rest.

○   ○   ○

We were all taken aback by this turn of events. We had expected her to live for another week or two, considering her condition during that night. We decided to call our brother Manuel on his cell phone to inform him of what had transpired, giving him the option to delay their arrival. However, since they were already more than halfway there, they decided to continue their journey. They reached us at around nine o'clock that night, only to find out that our mother had been sleeping, and it was likely she would continue to do so throughout the night. Consequently, my brother and his family came to my house to spend the night, with the plan to return to our mother's house in the morning.

The following morning, at around eight o'clock, I received a phone call from my sister Sonia. She informed me that our mother had passed away during the night. As I stood on the other end of the phone, a smile spread across my face, and I thought, *What a way to go!* I felt an overwhelming sense of peace and joy for her, knowing that she had transitioned in such a beautiful manner. It was a beautiful thing to witness how in the last several months of my mother's life, she truly lived them with a kingdom-minded spirit.

o   o   o

About six months after my mother's passing, I felt a strong calling from God to travel to Mexico and share the Gospel with her remaining siblings. Accompanied by my sister Sonia and brother Sam, we embarked on this mission to reach out to her family. Upon arriving, we were warmly welcomed by relatives we had not seen in fifteen years. During a family dinner, I took the opportunity to discuss salvation, especially after sharing the story of how my mother had passed.

As I spoke about how anyone can be saved through faith in Christ, my uncle (who was a bishop to the Catholic Church in Mexico) disagreed, stating that someone who committed grave sins like murder would not be saved. I explained that Jesus's sacrifice on the cross covers all sins, but the person must come to Christ in repentance. This discussion escalated, and I mentioned the apostle Paul, who, before his conversion, persecuted Christians but found redemption in Jesus. My uncle stated, "Paul did not kill a lot of people."

I then asked him, "How many people does one have to kill before the cross is not sufficient?"

Unfortunately, my uncle got angry, stood up, and said, "A person does not have to believe that Jesus was the Son of God to be saved," and left the room. It was disheartening to see my uncle, who has spent most of his life devoted to the Catholic Church and who was so knowledgeable about its history, miss the fundamental truth of the Gospel.

I realized that this situation is not uncommon even today. Many people learn about the church's history or the origins of the Bible without delving into its teachings, missing the profound message of redemption and salvation found in the Gospel.

o   o   o

Months later as I was reflecting on my mother's peaceful passing, my thoughts turned to my own mortality. I pondered how my own journey might unfold when my time comes. Would I experience a serene departure like my mother, or would I endure the agonizing pain my father went through? Unfortunately, my father's passing was far from peaceful. My mother, my brother, and I were all present in the hospital room during his final moments. He had endured days of excruciating pain leading up to his passing. I could see his struggle to hold on until the very end, and it was a heartbreaking sight to witness. Death, for most people, is an uncomfortable subject. Even though we are aware that death is inevitable, we tend to avoid discussing it, for the mere thought of our own mortality can be unsettling.

o   o   o

Among the many characters in the Bible, one of my favorites is Enoch. Although he is not widely known due to the limited mention of him in the Bible, I greatly admire him for his relationship with God. I like to think that it was the birth of his son Methuselah that played a significant role in Enoch's desire to seek God. This resonated with my own journey. It was after the birth of my son that I began to grasp the depth of God's love for us as a father and the reasons behind his rules and guidelines—all rooted in his immense love for us. With the birth of my son, my longing to know God grew, and as I delved deeper into my relationship with him, I gained a greater understanding of his character.

Genesis 5:21–24 (NIV) recounts Enoch's story:

> When Enoch had lived 65 years, he became the father of Methuselah. And after he became the father of Methuselah, Enoch walked with God 300 years and had other sons and daughters. Altogether, Enoch lived 365 years. Enoch walked with God; then he was no more, because God took him away.

Enoch's unwavering walk with God is something that deeply inspires me. He cultivated such a close relationship with God that Enoch walked alongside him for a remarkable three hundred years. Notice the Bible does not say that God walked with Enoch, which is very important to understand. And in the end, God took him away, and he was no more. This brief account portrays the extraordinary connection Enoch had with the divine, ultimately leading to his departure from this earthly realm without experiencing death.

Indeed, many people are familiar with the story of Elijah being taken up to heaven without experiencing death, but Enoch shares a similar fate. Enoch's narrative reveals that he walked with God, emphasizing that it was Enoch who aligned himself with God's path rather than the other way around. Most of us live a life where we go where we want to go, and when we find ourselves in need, then we call on God. Walking with someone implies ongoing communication and companionship, and this is how I strive to live my life. I endeavor to maintain a continual dialogue with God throughout my day. Sometimes I have good days and sometimes not so good, but my hope and prayer are that as I near the end of my life, I will experience more and more days filled with goodness.

o   o   o

A story shared by J. Vernon McGee captured the essence of Enoch's close relationship with God. He recounted a tale he heard about a mother who asked her daughter in the car on their way home after attending church what she had learned in Sunday school class. The little girl responded, saying they learned about a man named Enoch. The mother had no idea who Enoch was, so she inquired further, asking what the lesson was about. The girl replied, "Well, every morning God would come by Enoch's house, and they would go for long walks."

On one occasion, as they walked and conversed, Enoch noticed the encroaching darkness and realized he should return home before he lost his way. But God responded, saying, "You know, Enoch, you are much closer to my house than you are to your own. Why don't you just come home with me?" This story beautifully captures the essence of Enoch's relationship with God.

Instead of fixating on how or when we will die, we should ask ourselves a different question: If today were my appointed time, would my life be closer to God's house or to my own? In other words, am I more focused on the kingdom of God or consumed by worldly matters? It is this kingdom-minded perspective that truly matters.

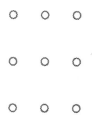

In case you were wondering about my father's salvation, like I mentioned earlier, during my father's final days, he endured a lot of suffering. At that time, I was a young Christian and unsure of how to share the Gospel effectively. So I reached out to Carl, a man from our church whom I admired for his zeal in witnessing to others. One weekend morning, Carl visited my father and graciously shared the Gospel with him. In response to the invitation, my father prayed alongside Carl and accepted Jesus into his life. It was a profound moment of faith and comfort during a difficult time.

CHAPTER 5

TIME IS RUNNING OUT!

In the early 1990s, when I was in my thirties, I found myself as a single parent raising my five-year-old son in a modest home. Living paycheck to paycheck, I accumulated some credit card debt and fell two years behind on my homeowners' association (HOA) payments. Every few months, I received stern letters reminding me of my failure to adhere to certain bylaws (which I never bothered to look up) and demanding full payment for last year's and this year's HOA bills. Then one day a certified letter arrived, warning me that if I did not catch up on my HOA payments within thirty days, my house would be put up for auction. Instead of seeking legal advice to verify the validity of the situation, I turned to a few people whom I considered smarter than myself. One particular friend whom I believed to be highly intelligent assured me, "Daniel, do you really think they can auction off your house just because you're behind on your HOA bill? It's just a scare tactic to get you to pay." Satisfied with that response, along with my other friends who told me pretty much the same thing, I did not pursue legal counsel.

Around thirty days later, one evening after my son's baseball practice, we arrived home to find a note taped to the front door. I read it, and it essentially said, "Hello, my name is so-and-so, and we have just purchased your home. To save money, please do not make any further house payments to your mortgage company. Also, we request that you vacate the residence within ninety days as we will be putting your house on the market." My heart sank, and I felt a pit in my stomach all night. Sleep eluded me. The following morning, I finally sought legal advice, but it was too late—the house was no longer mine.

○   ○   ○

Regrettably, many people behave similarly when it comes to our salvation. They allow people to persuade them with statements like, "If there is a God, do you really think he would send a good person to hell?" Instead of relying on what scripture actually says, they rely on their feelings. A prime example of this was the conversation I mentioned in chapter 2 between Joel Osteen and Oprah. Neither Oprah nor Joel cared about the truth. Oprah wanted Joel to validate her feelings (which is often what many of us do when faced with a moral challenge that we know deep down inside contradicts what the Bible teaches: we go to the one person who we know will validate what we are seeking), and Joel, wanting to maintain his popularity, told her exactly what she wanted to hear. The Bible is the only religious text that teaches us about the deceitfulness of our own hearts.

Jeremiah 17:9 (NIV) states, "The heart is deceitful above all things and beyond cure. Who can understand it?"

To stand firm in truth and righteousness, we must recognize the deceitful nature of our hearts and seek the truth so that we can stand for truth. Relying solely on our feelings can lead us astray. Consider the following example: Imagine encountering a person on the verge of starvation. Our instinctive feelings might urge us to provide a large meal immediately. However, unbeknownst to us, reintroducing food too quickly after prolonged starvation or malnourishment can trigger a potentially fatal condition known as refeeding syndrome.

This scenario demonstrates the importance of seeking knowledge and wisdom before acting based on our emotions. We must diligently search for truth and educate ourselves to make informed decisions that align with God's truth. Remember Pastor Matt's words: fight for your heart so you can fight with your heart.

That is why Proverbs 4:23 (NIV) advises, "Above all else, guard your heart, for everything you do flows from it." The book of Proverbs urges us to protect our hearts, meaning we should not be deceived by popularity or emotions when it comes to discerning the truth. The only way to fight for what is true is by first learning what is true.

o   o   o

In this chapter, I will provide several scriptural reasons for why I believe that we are the generation destined to witness the return of Christ. Even though there are many more examples from scripture that I can use, I will keep it to only a select few to make my point; otherwise, this chapter alone will be as long as the first four combined. Now I understand, because I have brought up the topic of end times, that many of you may immediately recall the verse "No one knows the day or hour." This is the go-to verse that many people pull out of their holster (including my past self) whenever this topic arises. However, what I have discovered about the people who use this verse is that they have rarely delved into the study of eschatology. They use this verse as a means to avoid the complexities of this challenging subject.

As you read through my examples, you have two choices: you can continue to rely on that verse as your fallback, or you can approach this with an open mind. While it is true that no one knows the day or the hour, it does not mean we cannot discern the season or the timing. Jesus himself has acknowledged that we can recognize the season. Moreover, we can discern the timing based on scripture. Consider this: if God did not want us to know the season or timing, wouldn't he have simply stated, "No one knows the month or year"? That would have settled the matter definitively.

Consider (Revelation 3:3 NIV) Remember, therefore, what you have received and heard; hold it fast, and repent. But if you do not wake up, I will come like a thief, and you will not know at what time I will come to you.

This verse emphasizes that if we fail to awaken spiritually, Jesus will arrive unexpectedly, like a thief. Therefore, it stands to reason that if we do awaken spiritually, we will be attuned to the signs of his coming. This is just one example, but there are several more that convey the same warning.

o   o   o

As we read scripture, we become aware that God is a God of order and significance, and numbers hold great importance in the Bible. For example, the number 7 represents perfection, the number 3 signifies divine wholeness, the number 10 denotes divine order. These are just a few examples, but there are numerous instances throughout scripture. My point is that God operates with numbers, a universal language.

Allow me to provide another illustration: In the Bible, we find instances where the number forty holds significant meaning. For instance, the story of Noah's Ark depicts forty days and forty nights of rain, while Moses spent forty days and nights atop Mount Sinai in communion with God. Furthermore, Jesus embarked on a forty-day fast, and Jonah went to Nineveh, proclaiming they had forty days to repent.

Now, can we simply dismiss these occurrences as mere coincidences? I think not. My perspective is that God operates with meticulous precision; He is a God of order, orchestrating events with specific timings. Even when God fashioned the sun and the stars, He imparted a profound purpose to them, as evidenced in Genesis 1:14 (NIV), where He declared, "let them serve as signs to mark sacred times."

I share this because I have encountered many who believe that Jesus could return at any moment, but I hold a different view. Allow me to offer some examples to explain:

Could Jesus have returned a few weeks after His ascension? No, for He foretold the suffering that His disciples would endure, which had to unfold first; otherwise, His word would have been inaccurate.

Could Jesus have returned two or three decades later after the disciples' suffering? Once again, no, as prophecy indicated the fall of Jerusalem and the scattering of the Jewish people.

Could Jesus return a century later or even a millennium? Again, the answer is no, for prophecy foresaw the rebirth of the Jewish nation, an event that materialized in 1948.

Could Jesus return tomorrow? No, as Paul informs us in 2 Thessalonians, the man of lawlessness (often identified as the antichrist) must be revealed first.

These examples underscore the idea that God's plan unfolds according to a divine timetable, marked by specific events and prophecies. It is a reminder that while we anticipate Christ's return, we must align our expectations with the intricate tapestry of God's design.

o   o   o

So how can I claim that we can know the timing? Well, in the book of Daniel, we are informed that the tribulation period will last for 7 years, with 1,260 days for the first half and 1,260 days for the second half. Some of you may be calculating and thinking, *Wait, 1,260 plus 1,260 equals 2,520, which when divided by 365 days does not yield 7 years but rather 6.9 years.* This is true, but it is essential to recognize that the calendar we currently use has deviated from God's calendar. The bible is not clear on how many days they used per calendar year, but there is evidence that certain cultures during that time did use a 360-day year, where each month consisted of thirty days. I tend to believe this because of the evidence found in the book of Enoch in the lost scrolls. However, there are also difference of opinions on how they adjusted it, to make up the difference like we do every leap year.

Furthermore, we have even modified the starting point of a new day. While we have been taught that a new day begins at midnight, according to the Bible, the new day commences at sunset. This is evident in the book of Genesis as God created each day, with the phrase "And there was evening, and there was morning—the first day."

Let us talk about the Sabbath, a subject that has often sparked debates and discussions among Christians. If you are to ask various believers when the Sabbath is, the majority of people will assert that the Sabbath is on Sunday as it has become the primary day of worship for Christians, following the examples set by the early church in the book of Acts. However, it is important to clarify that the original Sabbath day has remained unchanged throughout history—it has always been Saturday.

The biblical concept of the Sabbath finds its roots in the Creation story, where on the seventh day, God rested from his work of creating the world. This day of rest was later established as a sign of the covenant between God and the Israelites, and it became an integral part of their religious practices. Throughout the Old Testament, the Sabbath is consistently referred to as the seventh day of the week, or Saturday.

Now when we look at the New Testament, we see that the early Christians, particularly in the book of Acts, began to gather and worship on Sundays. This transition was influenced by the significance of the resurrection of Jesus Christ, which occurred on a Sunday. As the apostles spread the Gospel, they celebrated the Lord's Day, the day of Christ's resurrection, with joy and worship.

However, it's crucial to differentiate between the biblical Sabbath day, which remains on Saturday, and the Christian tradition of gathering for worship on Sunday, the Lord's Day. The distinction between the two is essential to avoid confusion.

o   o   o

Even though we are not explicitly informed about when the tribulation will commence, we are given a significant sign that will occur at its midpoint—"the abomination that causes desolation." This event occurs when the Antichrist is revealed, entering the temple, ceasing the daily sacrifices, and proclaiming himself as God. When this happens, we can identify that we have reached the midpoint of the tribulation.

For those who hold the belief of the pretribulation rapture, I invite you to consider the words of Paul in 2 Thessalonians 2:1–3 (NIV). In this passage, Paul addresses the concerns of the Thessalonians who may have believed they had missed the rapture and were left behind. It is important to closely examine what Paul writes:

> Concerning the coming of our Lord Jesus Christ and our being gathered to him, we ask you, brothers and sisters, not to become easily unsettled or alarmed by the teaching allegedly from us—whether by a prophecy or by word of mouth or by letter—asserting that the day of the Lord has already come. Don't let anyone deceive you in any way, for that day will not come until the rebellion occurs and the man of lawlessness is revealed, the man doomed to destruction.

Paul's intention is to reassure the Thessalonians and prevent them from being swayed by false teachings. He emphasizes that the day of the Lord, which includes the gathering of believers to Jesus, has not yet come. He specifically states that before that day can occur, two significant events must take place: the rebellion and the revelation of the man of lawlessness, who is commonly understood to be the Antichrist. According to scriptural evidence, the unveiling of the Antichrist will happen at the midpoint of the tribulation.

This passage serves as a reminder that the timing of the rapture and the events surrounding it are intricately linked to the unfolding of God's plan in the end times. It encourages believers to remain steadfast and not be easily swayed by claims that the rapture will happen at the beginning of the tribulation. Instead, we are called to hold on to the truth of scripture and remain vigilant, knowing that certain events must occur before the day of the Lord and our gathering to Jesus can transpire.

o o o

Now let us revisit the verse from the book of Matthew where Jesus says, "No one knows the day or hour." Now did you know that this is not exactly what Jesus has said, even though many people who use that verse quote it that way? In reality, he states, "But about that day or hour no one knows, not even the angels in heaven, nor the Son, but only the Father" (NIV). This distinction brings a subtle change in understanding. Jesus is indicating that the precise moment of his return remains unknown, and I agree with this perspective.

Did you also know that immediately after Jesus made that statement, he shared the parable of the ten virgins? I consider these verses to be the third of the three most sobering verses that should cause all believers to take Paul's advice and examine ourselves. Allow me to recount it:

> At that time, the kingdom of heaven will be like ten virgins who took their lamps and went out to meet the bridegroom. Five of them were foolish, and five were wise. The foolish ones took their lamps but did not bring any oil with them, while the wise ones took oil in jars along with their lamps. The bridegroom was delayed, and they all became drowsy and fell asleep.
>
> At midnight, the cry rang out, "Here's the bridegroom! Come out to meet him!"
>
> Then all the virgins woke up and trimmed their lamps. The foolish ones said to the wise, "Give us some of your oil, for our lamps are going out."
>
> But the wise replied, "No, there may not be enough for both us and you. Instead, go to those who sell oil and buy some for yourselves."
>
> While they went to buy the oil, the bridegroom arrived. The virgins who were ready went in with him to the wedding banquet, and the door was shut.
>
> Later, the other virgins came and pleaded, "Lord, Lord, open the door for us!"
>
> But he replied, "Truly I tell you, I do not know you."
>
> Therefore, keep watch, because you do not know the day or the hour. Matthew 25:1-13 (NIV)

Observe the presence of five wise and five foolish virgins in the parable. I believe the wise represent those who have the Holy Spirit which makes them true followers of Christ, while the foolish are those who mistakenly believe they are in good standing with God due to their works, but in reality, they are not. Oil in the Bible represents an anointment; believers are anointed/sealed by the Holy Spirit. As we have discussed earlier, God considers someone a fool when they place their trust solely in worldly accomplishments. The five foolish virgins have staked their entry into the wedding banquet on their own good deeds. This reliance on works is evident in Jesus' earlier words in Matthew:

"Many will say to me on that day, 'Lord, Lord, did we not prophesy in your name and in your name drive out demons and in your name perform many miracles?' Then I will tell them plainly, 'I never knew you. Away from me, you evildoers!' Matthew 7:22-23, (NIV).

These two parables are one of the same, since we know this happens "On that day" which is the day of Christ's return.

It is noteworthy that their entire plea revolves around works, with no acknowledgment of placing trust in the redemptive work of Jesus on the cross. Trusting in what Jesus accomplished on the cross entails making Him the Lord of one's life, the central axis around which our lives turn.

This passage is alarming for believers for two significant reasons:

1. The five foolish virgins did not fall for the great illusion, nor did they submit to the mark of the beast. They diligently awaited the Lord's return, only to be met with the unsettling words, "I never knew you. Away from me, you evildoers!"
2. The staggering reality is the sheer number of people who make it to the end, only to be denied—an unsettling half of them.

It is also noteworthy that all ten virgins have gone out at the appropriate time. How is this possible? It can be attributed to their ability to piece together the signs in the sky and events transpiring in the world during the end times, which has enabled them to anticipate the return of Jesus. Furthermore, even though the five wise virgins have not accurately pinpointed the exact day or hour, they have only missed it by a margin of less than a day.

Did you observe that the five foolish virgins arrive after the door has been shut? Why? It is because they have been preoccupied with trying to buy oil, which is something that cannot be bought. There are people who may choose to leave Christianity because they struggle with the concept that salvation cannot be earned through personal accomplishments. They desire to achieve and accomplish great things to validate their worth and find fulfillment. Perhaps this is why the five wise virgins in the parable advise the foolish ones to go buy oil as they may have wanted to hear a task or action, they can perform to secure their place.

We can find a similar pattern in the story of Naaman in the Old Testament. When the prophet Elisha instructed Naaman to dip himself in the Jordan River seven times to be healed of his leprosy, Naaman became angry. Naaman was a commander of the armies of Ben-Hadad; maybe that was why he expected a grand gesture or a heroic feat rather than a seemingly simple act of obedience.

These instances highlight a common tendency among some people to seek validation and significance through their own achievements. They struggle with the idea that salvation is a gift from God, received through faith, rather than something that can be earned through personal accomplishments or deeds. The message of grace challenges their desire for self-sufficiency and the need to feel in control.

It is important to understand that in Christianity, salvation is not about what we can do to earn our way to heaven but rather about placing our trust and faith in Jesus Christ, who has already accomplished everything on our behalf on the way he has lived, then finalized it on the cross. It is through his sacrifice and grace that we find redemption and eternal life. Embracing this truth requires humility and a shift in perspective, recognizing that our worth and identity are found in Christ, not in our own accomplishments.

O   O   O

Jesus likened the end times to the days of Noah. One of those examples of those days is that once the door to the ark was closed, time had run out. It was too late for anyone else to enter.

Living a life centered on counting one's own works may lead someone to attend church, study scripture, and engage in godly activities, but it is not enough. When we place our trust solely in our good deeds, there is no motivation for us to confess our darkest sins to God. It does not foster humility but rather pride when we approach God as we believe he is pleased with our lifestyle. Pride is one of the greatest sins that keep one from attaining eternal life. This truth is illuminated in the parable that Jesus has told in Luke:

> To some who were confident of their own righteousness and looked down on everyone else, Jesus told this parable: "Two men went up to the temple to pray, one a Pharisee and the other a tax collector. The Pharisee stood by himself and prayed: 'God, I thank you that I am not like other people—robbers, evildoers, adulterers— or even like this tax collector. I fast twice a week and give a tenth of all I get.'
>
> "But the tax collector stood at a distance. He would not even look up to heaven, but beat his breast and said, 'God, have mercy on me, a sinner.'
>
> "I tell you that this man, rather than the other, went home justified before God. For all those who exalt themselves will be humbled, and those who humble themselves will be exalted." (Luke 18:9–14, NIV)

In this parable, the tax collector approaches God with humility. He is so overwhelmed with shame that he cannot even raise his eyes to heaven. He recognizes the severity of his condition and pleads for mercy, which those who come to God based on their good deeds and accomplishments fail to do. That is why Jesus can say, "I never knew you." To truly know someone, that person must be willing to share everything about themselves, which those who persist in foolishness do not.

o   o   o

Now let us consider the profound insights provided in Matthew 24:4–8 (NIV), where Jesus outlines a series of events that will unfold in the end times. Let us focus on the initial stages described by Jesus:

> Watch out that no one deceives you. For many will come in my name, claiming, "I am the Messiah," and will deceive many. You will hear of wars and rumors of wars, but see to it that you are not alarmed. Such things must happen, but the end is still to come. Nation will rise against nation, and kingdom against kingdom. There will be famines and earthquakes in various places. All these are the beginning of birth pains.

Could it be that these seemingly straightforward descriptions provide a key to identifying the onset of the tribulation? I think it may be. Often, scholars and teachers dismiss these verses by pointing to the ongoing presence of wars, false messiahs, and other calamities throughout history. While this is true, we must delve deeper into Jesus's words to grasp their full significance.

Why would Jesus mention wars and rumors of wars if they were already prevalent at the time he spoke these words? The answer lies in the specificity of these future events. Jesus is not referring to generic conflicts and false messiahs that have already occurred; he is alluding to distinct occurrences yet to come. We are anticipating a particular false messiah who will have a profound impact on the world stage.

Let us examine the text more closely. Jesus states, "For many will come in my name, claiming, 'I am the Messiah,' and will deceive many." Interestingly, the word *many* is used in both instances, but they carry different connotations. In the context of rare and exceptional occurrences, such as a renowned painting or the arrival of a messiah, *many* can refer to a dozen or even fewer. However, when applied to the

183

general population, *many* assumes a significantly larger scale. In this case, a few hundred will be considered a small number. Despite the presence of various self-proclaimed messiahs throughout history, we have yet to witness one who deceives a substantial portion of humanity. Therefore, when a false messiah emerges on the world stage and deceives hundreds of thousands, or even millions, of people, we can discern that we are somewhere in the first three and half years of the tribulation period. The wars and rumors of wars that follow may very well be ignited by the influence and actions of this false messiah. It is also worth noting that the false messiah does not have to be of Christian faith.

By carefully examining the text and its implications, we can gain deeper insights into the signs of the end times. It is important to approach these prophecies with a discerning mindset and remain vigilant for the specific events that Jesus has foretold. The emergence of a false messiah capable of deceiving a significant number of people will mark a crucial turning point, leading to further upheavals and conflicts. Therefore, let us be watchful and prepared for the fulfillment of these prophecies as we navigate the complexities of the present age.

○   ○   ○

Let us now delve into the significance of the seven feasts that God ordained in the book of Leviticus. By examining each feast, we can see how some of them have already been fulfilled in Jesus's first coming:

1. The Feast of Passover—Jesus died on this day.
2. The Feast of Unleavened Bread—Jesus was buried on this day.
3. The Feast of Firstfruits—Jesus was resurrected on this day.
4. The Feast of Pentecost—The Holy Spirit descended on the apostles on this day.
5. The Feast of Trumpets— Awaiting fulfillment.
6. The Feast of the Day of Atonement— Awaiting fulfillment.
7. The Feast of Tabernacles— Awaiting fulfillment.

Did you notice that the next feast awaiting fulfillment is the Feast of Trumpets? How did Jesus describe his return? In Matthew 24:30–31 (NIV), Jesus said:

> Then will appear the sign of the Son of Man in heaven. And then all the peoples of the earth will mourn when they see the Son of Man coming on the clouds of heaven, with power and great glory. And he will send his angels with a loud trumpet call, and they will gather his elect from the four winds, from one end of the heavens to the other."

Pay attention to the fact that when Jesus returns, there will be a loud trumpet call. Interestingly, the Feast of Trumpets is the only feast that spans two days. Did you also know that it was literally the only first that no one knew that day or hour. This feast begins with the sighting of the new moon, and in ancient times, without the aid of computers, two witnesses would go out to observe the timing. Upon sighting the new moon, they would sound the trumpet, signifying the start of the feast to everyone.

These connections highlight the significance of the Feast of Trumpets in relation to Jesus's return. The loud trumpet call and the mysterious nature of the feast align with the anticipation of his Second Coming.

It is important to note that the two witnesses mentioned earlier in the context of the Feast of Trumpets always had an understanding of the timing but not the precise day or hour. Their role was to be vigilant and observant, in tune with the signs and the sighting of the new moon that marked the beginning of the feast. While they had a general awareness of the timing, the exact time remained unknown.

While I may express a belief in Jesus' return aligning with the Feast of Trumpets, it's crucial to acknowledge Jesus' explicit statement that no one knows the day or hour, still remains true.

O   O   O

Before we delve into the verses that indicate we are the generation destined to witness the return of Jesus, it is crucial to grasp God's prophetic timing. In certain instances, when God refers to a day, he is actually alluding to a prophetic day, which symbolizes a span of one thousand years. We gain insight into this understanding from Psalm 90:4 (NIV), which states, "A thousand years in your sight are like a day that has just gone by, or like a watch in the night."

Furthermore, in 2 Peter 3:8, Peter emphasizes the importance of this concept:

> But do not forget this one thing, dear friends: With the
> Lord a day is like a thousand years, and a thousand years
> are like a day.

He urges us not to forget that "with the Lord, a day is like a thousand years, and a thousand years are like a day." This reminder is crucial because, to analyze and interpret prophecy, we sometimes need to apply this rule of God's time perspective.

Understanding God's prophetic timing, where a day can represent a thousand years and vice versa, provides us with a broader perspective when examining biblical prophecies related to the return of Jesus. It allows us to grasp the unfolding of events and their significance within God's divine timetable.

> In Isaiah 46:10 (NIV), it is written,
> I make known the end from the beginning,
> from ancient times, what is still to come.
> I say, "My purpose will stand,
> and I will do all that I please."

This intriguing phrase, "I make known the end from the beginning," raises thought-provoking possibilities. One interpretation can be that since the creation account in Genesis unfolds over seven days, it can symbolically represent a larger time frame of seven thousand years. According to this perspective, Jesus will return after about six thousand years (and according to scripture, our generation is at the end of the six thousand years), followed by a final thousand years where he reigns alongside believers—an envisioned millennial Sabbath.

○   ○   ○

While this concept may initially seem unconventional, it is worth noting that some early Christian scholars have held this belief. It offers an intriguing way to understand the relationship between the biblical account of creation and the unfolding of God's plan throughout history.

It is essential to approach such interpretations with an open mind, recognizing that understanding God's timing and his plans can be a complex and multifaceted endeavor. Exploring various perspectives helps us delve deeper into the mysteries of scripture and consider the rich tapestry of theological thought throughout history.

Here are a couple of examples of early Christians that held to this belief, but there are more.

> The Sabbath is mentioned at the beginning of the creation [thus]: "And God made in six days the works of His hands, and made an end on the seventh day, and rested on it, and sanctified it." Attend, my children, to the meaning of this expression, "He finished in six days." This implieth that the Lord will finish all things in six thousand years, for a day is with Him a thousand years. And He Himself testifieth, saying, "Behold, to-day will be as a thousand years." Therefore, my children, in six days, that is, in six thousand years, all things will be finished. "And He rested on the seventh day." This meaneth: when His Son, coming [again], shall destroy the time of the wicked man, and judge the ungodly, and change the sun, and the moon, and the stars, then shall He truly rest on the seventh day. (*Epistle: Barnabas,* fl. 177)

Now this was written sometime between AD 70 and 132.

For in as many days as this world was made, in so many thousand years shall it be concluded. And for this reason the <u>Scripture</u> says: Thus the heaven and the earth were finished, and all their adornment. And God brought to a conclusion upon the sixth day the works that He had made; and God rested upon the seventh day from all His works. This is an account of the things formerly created, as also it is a <u>prophecy</u> of what is to come. For the day of the Lord is as a thousand years; and in six days <u>created</u> things were completed: it is evident, therefore, that they will come to an end at the sixth thousand year." (Irenaeus, 150)

This was written in around AD 180.

o   o   o

Looking at certain scriptures through the lens of a thousand years can provide a deeper understanding compared with interpreting them as twenty-four-hour days. Let us consider a couple of examples.

In the book of Genesis, God warned Adam not to eat from the tree of knowledge, stating that in the day he ate from it, he would surely die.

But of the tree of the knowledge of good and evil you shall not eat, for in the day that you eat of it you shall surely die. (Genesis 2:17, NKJV)

However, we know that Adam did not physically die on that same day. Instead, we have been taught that he experienced spiritual death. Could it be that God, who understands the concept of a thousand years, made this statement while Satan perceived it as merely a twenty-four-hour day? Satan, desiring to destroy humanity, might have assumed that

Adam and Eve would perish within a literal twenty-four-hour period, therefore ending humanity.

So when did Adam die? Applying the principle of a thousand years, we can find significance in Adam's death occurring at the end of that first day when he lived for 930 years. Is this a mere coincidence, or have we overlooked the reminder provided by Peter?

O   O   O

It is interesting to note that when Adam and Eve were expelled from the Garden of Eden, it was not solely because they had eaten from the forbidden tree. Rather, they were kicked out to prevent them from eating from the tree of life as doing so would have allowed them to live beyond a single day, a thousand years.

> And the Lord God said, "The man has now become like one of us, knowing good and evil. He must not be allowed to reach out his hand and take also from the tree of life and eat, and live forever." So the Lord God banished him from the Garden of Eden to work the ground from which he had been taken. (Genesis 3:22–23, NIV)

By considering the concept of a thousand years in our interpretation of certain scriptures, we gain fresh insights and recognize the intricacies of God's timing and divine plan. It is crucial to understand that there are two prophetic principles regarding time. I have already explained the "day to a thousand years" principle, but there is also the prophetic "day to a year" principle found in

> the Bible, which we will now explore.
> In Zechariah 13:7 (NKJV), the scripture states,
> "Awake, O sword, against My Shepherd,
> Against the Man who is My Companion,"
> Says the LORD of hosts.
> "Strike the Shepherd,

> And the sheep will be scattered;
> Then I will turn My hand against the little ones."

We could all agree that the shepherd mentioned here referred to Jesus, and it was evident that forty years after Jesus was crucified, the Jewish people, symbolized as the sheep, were conquered and scattered throughout the known world. This aligned with the significance of the number 40 in biblical prophecy. Moreover, when the Pharisees asked Jesus for a sign, he referred to the sign of Jonah. One of the signs was when Jonah went to Nineveh and warned the people of their impending destruction within forty days. Jesus, by mentioning the sign of Jonah, indicated that the Pharisees had forty years to repent. The destruction of the city of Jerusalem in AD 70 corresponded to the completion of this prophetic timeline, validating the day-to-year prophetic principle.

Considering Jesus was likely crucified in AD 30, as widely believed by many scholars, including myself, it aligns with the day-to-year prophetic prophecy. God does not act randomly but works with divine order and symbolism as he is a God of numbers. These patterns and timelines were established from the very beginning, reflecting his meticulous plan.

o　o　o

Let us now explore Hosea 6:1–2 (NIV):
Come, let us return to the LORD.
He has torn us to pieces
but he will heal us;
he has injured us
but he will bind up our wounds.
After two days he will revive us;
on the third day he will restore us,
that we may live in his presence.

When we consider the events after Jesus's crucifixion, we know that the Jewish people were not immediately healed after two days, nor were they raised on the third day to live in his presence. However, when we apply the principle of a day representing a thousand years, a different perspective emerges.

If we consider that Jesus was crucified in AD 30, and we add the first "day" of a thousand years, we arrive at the year 1030. Adding the second "day" of a thousand years brings us to 2030. So what occurred after two days but before the third day? In 1948, the Jewish people reestablished their nation, a significant revival that aligns with Hosea's prophecy ("After two days will he revive us"). Now when Jesus returns for his Second Coming, scripture indicates that he will reign for one thousand years. This corresponds to the "third day," which is a symbolic representation of a thousand years. Thus, in 2030, as the third day, scripture states that he will raise us (referring to the rapture), and we shall live in his sight, which will be for a thousand years.

Now do I believe that Jesus will return in the year 2030? Maybe, but we still can discover something that may alter it a year or two, but my belief is 2030. We will be more certain when we come to the midpoint of the tribulation, as I've mentioned before, for there will be clear evidence of this.

○ ○ ○

Now let us examine another prophecy that points to Jesus's return timing aligning with the year 2030. In this prophecy, we do not need to rely on the principles of prophetic days or years.

In Matthew 24:3 (NIV), the disciples privately approached Jesus while he was sitting on the Mount of Olives, asking him about the sign of his coming and the end of the age. As we continued reading verses 4–31, Jesus described the events that would occur leading up to his return. Then in verses 32–34 (NIV), he shared a significant lesson:

> Now learn this lesson from the fig tree: As soon as its twigs get tender and its leaves come out, you know that summer is near. Even so, when you see all these things, you know that it is near, right at the door. Truly I tell you, this generation will certainly not pass away until all these things have happened.

To understand the context of this verse, we need to look at what happened before Jesus instructed his disciples to learn from the fig tree. Throughout the Bible, the fig tree symbolized Israel, representing the Jewish people. In the book of Mark, we gained insight into the significance of the prior day and that morning.

On the previous day (Mark 11:12–13), Jesus, feeling hungry, approached a fig tree in leaf but found no fruit since it was not the season for figs. He cursed the tree, and his disciples witnessed this. He then entered Jerusalem and discovered that the temple had been turned into a den of robbers. Jesus overturned the tables and pronounced a curse on the Pharisees by saying in Matthew 23:39 (NIV),

> For I tell you, you will not see me again until you say,
> "Blessed is he who comes in the name of the Lord."

On the same morning in Mark 11:20–22 (NIV), as they passed by the fig tree, the disciples noticed that it had withered from the roots up. Peter pointed this out to Jesus, who responded, "Have faith in God."

When Jesus instructed the disciples to learn from the fig tree, it would be important to note that on that very morning, they witnessed the fig tree that Jesus had cursed the day before withering away. So when Jesus mentioned the leaves coming out, it could symbolize the reestablishment of Israel as a nation in 1948. When he said, "This generation will not pass away," he referred to the generation of 1948.

While some scholars have referred to other passages in the Bible that mention the length of a generation as either 80 or 120 years, those examples pertain to the specific generation being discussed by the respective writers. Since Jesus explicitly refers to "this generation," we should consider the generation of Jewish people today. When we search for the average life span of Jewish people in Jerusalem, we find about 84 years for females and around 79 years for males, with an average of 82. Adding 82 years to 1948 brings us to the year 2030.

Consider this: Nineveh had 40 days to repent, and they chose repentance, avoiding destruction. In contrast, Israel had 40 years to repent, warned of the impending destruction of their city and scattering of the people. Unfortunately, they did not heed the warning, and the prophecy was fulfilled. Intriguingly, from the time of Israel's destruction in 70 AD until the year 2030 spans exactly 40 Jubilees. Is this mere coincidence? I leave that judgment to you.

o   o   o

One of the things that I find interesting is how remarkable it is to witness these revelations unfolding in our generation. It is as if these passages have been hidden in plain sight for two thousand years, and now they are being illuminated for us to understand.

As I mentioned earlier, these examples from the Bible are just a glimpse into the signs that point toward this generation. I encourage you to embark on your own research and exploration, delving deeper into this matter. Not only will it provide you with further insights but my sincere hope is that it will also deepen your relationship with God the Father and his Son, Jesus, through the Holy Spirit.

o   o   o

Even if my interpretation of end times turns out to be inaccurate (which is possible), there are three indisputable truths that remain:

1. This is not a Salvation Issue: It is crucial to recognize that differing opinions on end times are not salvation issues. My perspective on prophecy is just that—my perspective. If I, or others who hold different views, happen to be mistaken, it will not alter our ultimate goal of hearing the cherished words, "well done, good and faithful servant."
2. Core Beliefs Remain: The essence of what I have shared in chapters one through four remains unaltered. These core beliefs touch upon salvation, prompting us to continually examine our faith and its authenticity.
3. Time is Precious: Time is still running out for each of us. We cannot guarantee another day or even another moment. When people face God, many assume they have more time on Earth.

Time is a precious commodity; no one can make or maintain one moment. It all comes to us as a pure gift, so we must align our priorities accordingly. How we spend our time can have eternal consequences.

In summary, regardless of our views on end times, let us remember the enduring importance of our faith, the fleeting nature of time, and the imperative to align our priorities with an eternal perspective.

Jesus is indeed coming, and he will come as a righteous judge. When the trumpet sounds, it will be too late to make a decision. The door to the wedding banquet will be closed, and those without true faith will be left outside.

○   ○   ○

Now let me end this by pointing out a significant issue within Christianity - the tendency for believers to attack fellow believers especially over non-salvation matters. It is disheartening how often Christians lash out against one another due to disagreements on various doctrines. Countless times, I have encountered hurtful and evil words along with negative posts directed at others just because of differing opinions, even when those opinions are not tied to salvation matters.

Within the pages of this book, it is likely that readers will find themselves at odds with my views on topics like the timing of Christ's return and the concept of the Rapture. It is important to note that these two subjects do not pertain to salvation. Disagreement is permissible, and civil discussions where both parties can maintain their differing opinions even after the discourse are entirely acceptable. What is paramount, however, is how these disagreements are handled.

The love of Jesus should be evident in all our actions, including how we express our differences. It is puzzling how hatred and spite can emerge from the mouths and posts of those who claim to embody Christ's love. In the grand scheme, one of us - or perhaps both - might eventually realize our stance was incorrect. In such situations, I would rather exhibit humility while disagreeing or debating with a fellow believer, only to learn later that I was wrong. This is more preferable than feeling vindicated by using malicious words, only to later discover that the person I attacked had the correct perspective.

When we resort to evil or hateful words against fellow believers, or even non-believers, it is crucial to reflect on the source of those words. Are these words a result of our passion for upholding the Gospel? Not likely. These instances are not rooted in spreading the Good News. So, where do these words stem from? We should recall the wisdom of Jesus: "Out of the overflow of the heart, the mouth speaks." Such words come from the darkness harbored within our hearts.

My prayer is that everyone who reads this book will evaluate their lives and examine whether they truly are in the faith. Each person has the opportunity to make a commitment to seek a more intimate knowledge of God and Jesus. By doing so, when the time comes to stand before God, they will not be facing a stranger but a God whom they intimately know. May they hear those precious words "Well done, my good and faithful servant."

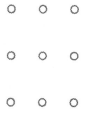

If you are curious about the outcome of the house I've lost, let me share the remarkable turn of events that unfolded: Upon discovering the note on the door with the address of the new owner, I wasted no time in reaching out to them. I crafted a heartfelt letter, expressing my desire to meet and discuss the situation. To my surprise, about a week later, I received a phone call from the new owner, expressing their willingness to meet with me at my house.

Several days passed, and the new owner, accompanied by his spouse, visited my house for the long-awaited meeting. Together with my son, we engaged in heartfelt discussions and negotiations. Remarkably, we were able to devise a payment plan agreement that would span two years. I committed to sending them monthly payments to cover most of the cost that they would have made as profit, after they sold the house.

It was revealed during our conversation that the new owners never met with the previous owners after purchasing a property from an auction as they aimed to maintain a business-driven approach devoid of emotional attachment. However, my letter had a profound impact on them, compelling them to make an exception. While I could not recall the exact words I wrote, I firmly believe that it was a true blessing from God that touched their hearts.

You may wonder how I managed to handle the financial responsibilities of my house payments and the additional payment to the new owners. During this time, my son and I temporarily moved into my sister-in-law's house for a period of two years. Meanwhile, I chose to rent out my own house, and the rental income proved sufficient to cover the new payment along with a small surplus each month.

With unwavering determination and the support of my son, I am delighted to share that after the designated two-year period, we were able to reclaim our beloved home. It was a joyous moment, knowing that through perseverance and the grace of God, we had overcome the challenges and regained what I foolishly lost.

This experience serves as a testament to the power of hope and resilience and the unexpected blessings that can manifest in our lives. It is a reminder that even in the midst of adversity, there is God working for good with the potential for a positive outcome.

Printed in the United States
by Baker & Taylor Publisher Services